dazzling bodies

dazzling bodies

Rethinking Spirituality
and Community Formation

Richard Valantasis

CASCADE *Books* • Eugene, Oregon

DAZZLING BODIES
Rethinking Spirituality and Community Formation

Copyright © 2014 Richard Valantasis. All rights reserved. Except for brief quotations in critical publications or reviews, no part of this book may be reproduced in any manner without prior written permission from the publisher. Write: Permissions, Wipf and Stock Publishers, 199 W. 8th Ave., Suite 3, Eugene, OR 97401.

Cascade Books
An Imprint of Wipf and Stock Publishers
199 W. 8th Ave., Suite 3
Eugene, OR 97401

www.wipfandstock.com

ISBN 13: 978-1-62564-780-1

Cataloging-in-Publication data:

Valantasis, Richard, 1946–

Dazzling bodies : rethinking spirituality and community formation / Richard Valantasis.

xviii + 118 p. ; 23 cm—Includes bibliographical references (109–10).

ISBN 13: 978-1-62564-780-1

1. Spiritual formation. 2. Communities—Religious aspects—Christianity. 3. Spiritual formation—Episcopal Church. 4. Spiritual formation—Orthodox Eastern Church. I. Title.

BV4511 V35 2014

Manufactured in the U.S.A.

For
Constance Delzell
Sally Brown
Doug Bleyle
Dan Handschy
Jennifer Phillips
Paxton Bleyle
Alan Fleischauer

Contents

Preface

THIS BOOK ARISES FROM three frustrations. Each commands some attention, and together they compel some thought.

First, I begin with a question. Why is it that perfectly vital and fine parishes fall apart after extending a call to a new minister who does not seem to fit the parish despite the valiant work of a search committee to find a suitable leader? This has happened more often than I like to think. Parishes seem not to know how to interview a potential ordained minister for their congregation, nor do they understand what criteria they must use to discern the right fit of leadership and parish identity. Somehow communication fails to produce the kind of conversations that allow solid discernment to happen. This book lays out a basis for talking about corporate spiritual formation that, I think, will assist parishes in understanding the way power is modulated in their midst, especially by their ordained leadership. It will also, I hope, provide some means of analyzing how religious communities sustain their sense of solidarity and identity.

Second, I have been frustrated for years about the way that *spirituality* has been sold to the American (and Western European) world as an individual set of practices divorced of community. The vast number of books that have been produced and sold under the category spirituality give the impression that all a person needs is a little time alone, away from family and others, and an inclination to search out the deepest part of one's self. These spirituality handbooks are designed primarily for people who want to get away from organized religion and explore the inner psychospiritual world in a vacuum. I could almost identify the American propensity for self-help with spirituality and would be hard-pressed to distinguish them. Throughout the history of Christian spirituality (and probably most others as well), however, spirituality has been intimately connected to communities. One's personal exploration of the life of the spirit grew out of community and fed the community out of which spiritual practices arose. The traditional Western spiritual practices arose in intentional communities such as monasteries or communities of preachers or sodalities of women and men dedicated to the ministry to the poor and the sick. In the context of Western religious history, spiritual practices (what we call simply spirituality) emerged from the formation proper to a community's mission and life. Spiritual practices linked the individual to a corporate mission by providing the means whereby an individual person could become a member of a community capable and empowered to live out the community's vocation. Spirituality, then, from the long perspective of Christian tradition, is not just for individuals, but for individuals intimately related to specific communities of religious practitioners. The contemporary disconnect between spirituality and community is a major frustration.

The third frustration that resulted in this book relates to common understanding of religious community life. Again, because American (and Western European) people are so oriented to understanding themselves as isolated and unique individuals, our understanding of the riches of communal living has suffered. Most people have a very flat understanding of community as a group of people who gather together for the enhancement of the lives of each individual person. Our tendency is to understand a group of people as merely an enhancement of the individual person. We look first to individuals and try from them to understand group dynamics. Having grown up in an ethnic culture in which community life and identity is primary, I have always understood community as something larger than the individual, and something more comprehensive in providing a variety of identities and perspectives. Community is complex: teeming with contradictions and conflicts, capable of galvanizing even mortal enemies into a cohesive society; with a corporate identity as rich and varied as any personal one, a community may work toward the health or destruction of groups and of individuals.

These three frustrations surfaced dramatically during my first parish-ministry assignment in a small New England congregation. The most exasperating part of being a parish minister was trying to figure out what was really going on in my parish. My seminary taught me many things

about Scripture, church history, church and society, ethics, pastoral counseling, preaching, and liturgy—you know all the categories covered both
in theological curricula and in ecclesiastical examinations. I had learned
these things well, and had even begun to consider how I should apply these
in the life of my first parish. The one thing I had not been taught—in fact it
was never even discussed—was how to understand and analyze the parish
as a community, or how to understand spiritual formation of individuals to
live in a parish community. I had learned how to do community things, but
I had not learned any means of analyzing the life of the community or of
integrating individuals into parish life. In order to assimilate those things
that I had learned, and in order to apply the knowledge I had acquired at
seminary to a parish's corporate formation, I needed first to gain an understanding of the corporate life of the people among whom I ministered.
I needed to understand not only spirituality or spiritual practices, but also
how those practices related to community life. I needed, in short, to rethink
spirituality and community from a critical perspective in order to connect
community formation with traditional spiritual practices. It was this dynamic that was missing for me, which I am now addressing in this book.

Many years later, after I had finished my doctorate and combined academic work with parish ministry in a parish in Boston, I taught a course at
Harvard Divinity School titled Liturgy and Spirituality. Because the course
had the word *spirituality* in the title, I attracted good students. All students
wanted to improve themselves and explore their inner lives. When they
read the syllabus, however, they were distressed that they would need to
read critical theory (in this case semiotics and social semiotics) as a lens
through which to understand dynamics of spiritual formation in community through analyzing liturgical practices. For the record, semiotics is
simply the study of communication systems through signs such as words,
gestures, sounds, and anything else capable of communicating through any
medium; social semiotics investigates the social dimension of communication by plotting systems of solidarity and power in social settings. I insisted
that the class participants learn a set of theories, difficult theories at that,
in order to explore the relationship of corporate worship to the corporate
spiritual life of the parish. They all struggled with it but slowly began to
master the difficult theories as lenses through which to analyze and understand liturgical communication.

Many, many years later a student in that class called me when she had
heard that I was taking a new position in the region where she lived. The

call was amazing. I had not heard from this woman since the time of this peculiar course at Harvard Divinity School, and she said that it was the one course that she used more than any other from her study. I asked her why. She replied that the exercise of consistent and thorough corporate analysis enabled her ministry to address directly and clearly the major issues, desires, yearnings, problems, and crises of the parish to which she was called to minister. Theory enabled her ministry to be effective and fulfilling not only to herself, but also to the various parishes in which she ministered. Over these years, I too have used this theory to evaluate parishes, both as a priest who was called to lead, and as a regular member. This book comes out of the material of that course, which was so important to my students, refracted through many years of being a parish priest and being involved in various parishes.

The development of diagnostic tools enabled ministry both for me and for my students to progress and to fulfill the deepest desires of us all. In other words, the development of diagnostic tools enabled us all to understand the process of developing a spirituality while staying closely connected to our religious communities. The consideration of those diagnostic tools mandates my writing this book. I bring to this book a reflection on theorized practice over many years, not only in parishes and various church organizations, but also in monastic communities. I have been involved in corporate spiritual formation for most of my ministerial life. I have been involved in various communities as they attempt to mature spiritually not simply by attracting or enabling individual members to develop but by addressing their life together as a corporate body, the body of Christ. In helping communities to mature corporately, I have used the theories that I have studied in the academy as a means of exploring new territory, new language, new ideas, new perspectives on an important aspect of modern church life. Over the years, I have tried to communicate the theoretical material that stands behind these next few chapters clearly and simply, mostly by analyzing typical experiences in religious communal living and by presenting that material in a variety of circumstances such as in sermons, on retreats, in renewal programs, in academic lectures, and in adult-education programs. I now offer the fruits of that reflective practice for people in the church and to the wider audience who reads this book.

Where does spiritual practice meet community life? This is an important question. Although it did not at first seem obvious to me and to my students, the answer lay readily at hand: most dynamics of a parish find their expression in one form or another in the community's worship. Worship—liturgy—is the place where individual spiritual insight meets the spiritual insight of others and becomes something larger than all the individual spiritualities as a communal identity. In worship one not only sees the individuals but glimpses the corporate identity: the community's life as a whole. It might be through the structure of the liturgy itself, or through references to community problems and blessings in the sermon, or through cares and concerns raised in the community's intercessory prayer, or through the references in the liturgy to the community's relationship with the wider church and society, or through who is authorized in a community to pray these prayers and whether others are encouraged to enter into them. Liturgy is a complex locus of corporate and individual spiritualities. I cannot imagine a situation in a parish's life that does not break into and affect the liturgy as a sign of its life. By analyzing the performative aspect of community liturgy, one may begin to understand the lived religion of the community. By treating the liturgy as a sign of the community (that is, as a system of communication within a parish), a person will have a starting point for understanding the life of the community and the formative context of all its members. By examining the way liturgy enables members of a community to communicate with other members both present and absent, and by reviewing the way the liturgy gathers up and directs the community's communication with God, the participants in the community (including the minister or the leaders of a parish) may begin to understand both the problems and the vitality of a community's spiritual life. The liturgy functions as a window into the corporate soul of a parish or religious community.

Already language begins to fail to communicate the richness of what I intend to say. I refer here to my use of the terms *corporate body* and *corporate soul*. This book is about changing how we understand our bodies as individuals and how our bodies are united into corporate bodies and how our corporate bodies are knit together into a local, then a universal, body of Christ. But I want to explore not simply the body, but the dazzling bodies: the bodies enlivened, renewed, sanctified, and transformed by engaging in the worship of God. I want to view the dazzling body as a conglomerate of individual bodies made glistening by their corporate engagement with the Spirit that moves through them, and made luminous by their combined and communal relationship to God. Those dazzling bodies are the bodies of Christian people in, around, and through whom God activates and empowers. Those dazzling bodies become a spiritual offering, a fragrant offering to God, which not only transforms individuals into a dazzling corporate body but also through those dazzling bodies transforms both the church and the world.

In a sense, this book counters the tendency among church people (most especially ordained clergy, theologians, seminarians, and seminary professors) to produce ideal descriptions of parishes—ideals that are in fact not ever achievable by most parishes. The ideal descriptions often relate to the articulation of a theology of parish life and are generally articulated as goals for community conduct of life and ministry. I certainly do not discourage theological formulations of parish life, but I encourage a kind of analysis of parish life that assesses the parish's achievement. Once a goal is set, the minister and congregants need some means of evaluating the progress in achieving the goal, and this book provides one means of that assessment. I use the term *dazzling bodies* as a means of pointing not so much to the conceptualizing of those theological goals but to the intentional spiritualizing of the corporate body through worship and common theological work. *Dazzling Bodies* points not to conceptual or theological work, but to the communicative activities that make Christian communities come to life.

The approach I take in this book also counters the tendency toward describing spirituality only through individual experiences. The language and the mode of contemporary spiritual studies focuses on an individual person's ability or capacity to be spiritual, so that spirituality addresses the psychospiritual practices of prayer and meditation of isolated individuals. My approach in this book focuses on the corporate dimension of spirituality. I do not deny the validity and importance of individual growth, but I emphasize that such growth generally takes place in community, in parishes and other religious groups that support individuals in their religious life. The corporate dimension in many respects creates the environment for individual growth, and it prepares the basis for people to grow together in their understanding of themselves, their society, their church, and their world. Corporate spiritual formation expands the purview of spirituality and engages the common work of members of a community for their mutual spiritual growth and development; corporate spiritual formation makes the various bodies dazzle. This is the reason for looking carefully at worship and liturgy, because the liturgy and other corporate devotional activities affect the lives of the participants. The liturgy affects different sorts of bodies—individual, social, and corporate—and acts upon each one of these to connect them to the presence and activity of God. Truly dazzling bodies emerge from their corporate engagement not only with other members of the body of Christ but also with the God made known in the community of faith. Such a perspective will change the way individual spiritual formation is described and understood.

Throughout the book, I use a technique of analyzing experience. It resembles a simplified and shortened case-study method. I wish to set the stage and provide skills for analyzing experience as it impinges on and results from corporate worship. The act of relating a narrative of an experience implicitly contains a method for its interpretation. We tell stories from a particular perspective that already betrays our systems of understanding. I recognize the shortcoming of such a method, but in the absence of widespread systems for analyzing corporate spiritual formation, this method sets the stage for using other methods for parish evaluation and analysis. I am convinced that delving into the analysis of individual and corporate experience becomes an important tool in ongoing spiritual formation. Social scientists, anthropologists, sociologists, and various other modern theorists provide other lenses, but the starting point for all of them seems to reside in the construction of a narrative descriptive of religious experience. That is where I usually begin.

This book is written for anyone who is interested in spirituality, but who has begun to have second thoughts about the myopia of the individual perspective in spirituality studies. It will be particularly important to lay leaders of a parish and to ministers who find themselves wanting to move beyond the current spirituality paradigm to something else, something more communal. The book arises out of my own experience as an Episcopal priest who has served a number of parishes and a variety of religious communities for over forty years. My conversation partners have been clergy and lay religious whose lives depend upon living in community and working toward a deeper and more mature spiritual practice. But my own perspective as a parish priest and chaplain does not limit the exploration of questions of corporate spiritual formation to professional religious leaders. While I wish to redress some of the harm done by avoiding corporate spiritual formation as part of the training of ministers and priests for their work, I recognize that these systems of analysis also have significance for any leader of a parish. Corporate spiritual formation is indeed a corporate function, so that any layperson who participates in liturgy needs also to understand how that participation transforms (both negatively and positively) each individual's life. Although the minister of a congregation usually bears the responsibility and authority for the corporate life of a community, the members of a community engage in corporate spiritual formation and should take a leading role in the formation and reformation of community spirituality. Both minister and active layperson will benefit by having initial conversations about corporate spiritual formation through the liturgy.

So what will this book do? This book will present in very simple language, using common ministerial experiences, an exploration of the nature of corporate spiritual formation through liturgy. The first chapter explores the culture within which ministry takes place and establishes the public aspect of spiritual formation. The second chapter introduces a simple theory of communication and a set of bodies that will become dazzling through discursive formation. This chapter lays the foundation for some easy lenses through which to understand a religious community. The third chapter explores the important dimension of forming a common language for prayer and liturgy. The fourth chapter analyzes the role and function of the sermon in community formation. The fifth chapter presents a theory of asceticism for guiding the formation of a person and community. The sixth chapter presents a series of examples of performances and practices for making the various bodies dazzle.

My goal for this book is to open the possibility for members of religious communities to become resplendent in their diverse communication with other members of their particular community, with God, and with the wider society. My goal is to enable bodies to become dazzling in their gloriously transfigured relationships with themselves, with their social worlds, and with the God whose radiance makes all things new. My goal is to make the work of the body of Christ when it gathers for worship an instrument for the renewal of the church.

Acknowledgments

I WOULD LIKE TO thank the gracious editors of *Sewanee Theological Review*, under the perceptive leadership of the Reverend Professor Christopher Bryan, who agreed to publish some of these chapters in their journal in anticipation of my completion of the whole project. I am grateful for their leadership in making this material available to the pastoral public, and I acknowledge that versions of chapters 1 and 2 originally appeared in their journal and have been revised for this book. They are used here with permission.

I would like also to acknowledge the community of ministers that made this book possible: the Sisters of the Society of Saint Margaret in the United States, who brought the question of corporate formation to the fore of my thinking; Jennifer Phillips, with whom I shared many of these experiences as co-rector of Saint John the Evangelist, Bowdoin Street, in Boston; Dan Handschy, who, while a student at Harvard, prepared for ordination by forming a community modeled on my "Eucharist and Community Life" paper, and who introduced this method as a system of formation in the Diocese of Missouri; Dudley Rose, the Associate Director of Ministerial Studies at Harvard Divinity School, with whom many of these concepts were explored in official departmental meetings and at Rosie's later; Vicki and Robert Sirota, whose passion for the life of the Spirit transformed these concepts into living ministerial life and the arts; and Janet Carlson, my wife, who has been a partner of over forty years in creating a household that indeed is a community of faith and a spiritual family of choice.

I dedicate this book to seven people who have made corporate spiritual formation through the liturgy a central part of their ministry. The Reverends Constance Delzell and Sally Brown transformed their parish by their singular faithfulness to the Anglican vision of a praying parish with an outward focus to mission. Week after week, through preaching, prayer, and the wonderful music of the liturgy, they formed a vital and living community as a model for the entire Diocese of Colorado.

Doug Bleyle, my student first at Iliff and then at Candler School of Theology at Emory University, came to me with a vision of corporate spiritual formation that animated his life. He challenged me to engage more quickly and articulately in corporate spiritual formation in my academic work and teaching. I hope I have honored his challenge.

Dan Handschy, after many years in a parish, has turned his mind now to formation of ministers in a doctoral program.

Jennifer Phillips has been a constant conversation partner about parish formation for many years, through good and bad times, and in a variety of parishes.

My three-year-old godson, Paxton Bleyle, represents yet another generation of those whose whole lives from birth onward have been lived in liturgical community. Paxton's ability to see God in community and in the eucharistic bread has brought me life. All six of these have provided me the impetus to think about these pressing issues for the church, and to begin to write about them.

Finally Alan Fleischauer, an incomparable friend, while at the gym kept asking me if I was yet finished with the book. Without his constant encouragement (some would say nagging), I would not have finished this project. Thank you, Alan; and thank you Connie, Sally, Doug, Dan, Jennifer, and Paxton.

1

Spirituality, Liturgy, and the Cultural Frame of Formation

SOME YEARS AGO, A former parishioner of mine asked her husband to invite me to visit her. She was in the hospital with a fever that seemed not to respond to treatment. Five years earlier she had been diagnosed with leukemia. After her initial illness she worked with the doctors, and her leukemia entered a remission. During those intervening years she was reasonably healthy, but now she had become sick again. She had decided that she would not, at this point in her illness, pursue any aggressive treatment, but that she would simply be made as comfortable as possible. She asked to see me because she needed to confirm for herself the theological basis of her decision. My former parish, and the parish that Mary and her family still attended, was between ministers, so I went to the interim minister to secure permission to relate pastorally to this family under these unusual circumstances.

Mary had been one of the laypeople in my former parish who was available during the day to carry on the ministry of the parish and to be available to help with weekday services. During the first two years in my first parish (as I have since discovered is usual), I buried most of the older generation. Each week, it seemed, we were celebrating the rites of Christian burial for the beloved older generation of the parish. At each of these services (and on the Sundays intervening) I preached what I perceived to be a basic Christian teaching about death and life in the Body of Christ and in the local community gathered weekly at the Eucharist to celebrate being that body. It was a simple gospel: Those who are baptized into Jesus Christ die with him and are raised to new life, a new life over which death has no more dominion. Those who have been baptized are invited to the Eucharist, which is the gathering of all people living and dead to celebrate the life of the resurrected Jesus in their midst. Those who have died and those who live are both perpetually living in the resurrected Jesus. Therefore, they are always connected and bound together until the last day when all will be gathered at the eternal heavenly banquet of which the local variety is an important but dim shadow. Mary remembered all these things, and she was convinced of them. She was willing to stake her life on them.

She called me to her hospital room simply to ask me if I still believed the gospel I had preached almost fifteen years earlier in my ministry. I assured her that indeed I did, and that I believed it even more as my years of experience in parish ministry continued. She explained that the resurrection theology developed in our community so many years earlier was the theology that would allow her to die peacefully when her time came, without necessarily working or praying for what would amount to a miraculous cure of a decidedly terminal illness. My covenant with her that day included a promise that I would be with her through her final hours, that I would help the family to understand the baptismal and eucharistic theology that had informed her life, and that I would assist the parish minister at her funeral.

Weeks passed. Twice I was called when she supposed she was nearing death, but both times it was simply a matter of her getting gradually weaker. We celebrated the Eucharist both times, with her husband and children present, during which we talked about the gospel—baptismal life, eucharistic fellowship, eternal life. Finally, in her last week, her family called to say that she was refusing medication according to her plan. I knew that this was the time to begin my work.

I went to see her, and we spoke alone for a long time. During this and the previous visit I explained to her in theological language and metaphor what would be happening to her body, the sorts of sensations that I have had described to me by many others with whom I sat while they died, and the kinds of visions, lights, and presences that would accompany her on her journey. I told Mary that it was like giving birth: you could pack the suitcase and put it at the door, but until it is time, nothing will help it along, and when it is time nothing can stop it. I described in detail what I knew from experience would be her final five or six hours.

At this particular meeting it was clear that she was very weak, but she was fully present, although obviously near death. Her three daughters and her husband were there as we celebrated the Eucharist. All we could gather for this impromptu service was a package of graham crackers and some cranberry juice. It was close enough. I spoke again, theologically, about the separation of soul and body, the gathering of those dying into a different life in the resurrected Jesus, and the meeting of saints living and dead in the Eucharist. Whenever they wanted to be close to their mother, all they needed to do, as we were doing then, was to come to the Eucharist. In this dim shadow of the final banquet all would be gathered. That evening we left; only one daughter would stay with her through the night.

The next day Mary became progressively weaker. It was decided that all the family would gather for a Eucharist that night. We agreed that the Eucharist would be celebrated at about seven-thirty in the evening. When I arrived at the hospital room, all of them were waiting. Mary was having difficulty talking, and greater difficulty breathing; but she was fully present. I read a portion of the high-priestly prayer from chapter 17 of John's gospel ("that all may be one") as the Scripture lesson and invited people to speak or pray as they felt called to do so. The children professed their love and gratitude for their mother; her husband repeatedly told her how much he loved her and how happy they were together; her brother spoke of a long and good relationship. Mary spoke of her love for each one. During this time Mary began to try to express some of her feelings—it was clear that she was no longer totally in her body, because her articulations were beyond her. She spoke of Jesus's presence, and that she needed to be released from the small things—not sins, not offenses—but some other small things that held her back. It was confused speech and confusing to hear. Her husband, brother, and children began gently to assure her of their release. Then, before this was entirely discussed, she announced that we had better hurry with the Eucharist. Her eyes were beginning to take on the look of one very near death. I prayed the eucharistic Great Thanksgiving, broke the bread, and dipped some of it into the wine and gave it to her, passing around the bread and the wine to the others. It was very intense. Mary was trying to rally to let people go home. She did, and they went on. Two daughters were to stay with her that night. The daughters reported to us that as soon as we all left Mary fell asleep. She did not again regain consciousness. The Eucharist with her family was her farewell.

I received a telephone call at about four o'clock in the morning and was told that the manner of her breathing had changed. There is a very specific sort of breathing pattern of those who are dying. The daughters said that she was still sleeping (the nurses called it a coma), but that she seemed comfortable. Once the breathing changed, I knew that Mary now was in control of her own dying. She would wait until everyone (including me) could gather again. When I got to school, I canceled all my afternoon appointments, attended one very important meeting, spoke with students who needed to talk with me that day, and then went to the hospital.

When I arrived, Mary was breathing the forced breathing of one working at keeping her body going. She had been breathing this way since about four that morning. When all the children assembled, we began to pray the litany for the dying, ending with the prayer for her grace-filled release from this life. Her breathing immediately slowed down, she became very peaceful, and her breathing was shallow but not strained. We recited the Twenty-Third Psalm, and everyone stood around her bed, touching her, speaking gently to her of our love, some crying. Her breathing slowed and, over the course of the next ten minutes or so, stopped. Quietly, she slipped away, only to join us whenever we gather at the Lord's Table.

This Narrative and Culture

I begin with this narrative because it provides a point of reference for reflection on the meaning of corporate spiritual formation through the liturgy: it provides the basis for studying the way Mary was formed as a religious person in a corporate setting, and how that formation became a new way of conceptualizing the world. The narrative also raises the question of the meaning of ministry and its relationship to spirituality. The lens through which I will examine this narrative comes from anthropology, because I wish to explore this and similar experiences from the perspective of culture, social relations, and individual personality.

Clifford Geertz explains that "culture is the fabric of meaning in terms of which human beings interpret their experience and guide their action," and that culture is "an ordered system of meaning and of symbols in terms of which social interaction takes place."[1] In my narrative above, there were actually a number of cultures present, even though they may not have been articulated: the medical culture, in which the body and its maladies are

1. Geertz, *Interpretation*, 144.
(1973)

4

defined, diagnosed, and treated, and in which the prolongation of life (independent of quality of life) is the primary objective; the religious culture, primarily located in a local religious community, which develops and promulgates an antique language of body and soul, of passing from one world to another, of sacraments and mysteries, and of eternal life; and the secular or popular American culture, which functions outside both the medical cultural frame and the theological cultural frame, and in which all things about sickness, dying, and loss of vitality are regularly denied or made invisible. There were probably other cultural systems available and operating at the same time, but these three are enough to begin our analysis.

Culture is the largest systematic referential base of human activity, thought, and emotions. Culture brings together the base metaphors that guide thinking and social relationships, and defines the nature and extent of familial relationships and social obligation. Culture demarcates the arenas of acceptability and social respectability, produces social and political unity and diversity by developing social solidarity and specifying the basis for exclusion, and defines the categories and referent of the real. In my narrative above, Mary chose the theological culture formed in our mutual parish life as the one she would use to explain her experience. Some in her family wanted her to continue using the medical culture so that she could fight the illness and prolong her life even for a short time. There was not a guarantee, moreover, that even clergy would be trained in a theological culture: Mary's experience of clergy was that not all of them understood the theological culture into which she had been formed through her engagement with her local parish; most pastoral counseling was modeled primarily on the language of the medical culture, lightly changed to reflect theological belief (that is, there was the potentiality for talking about God). I use the term *culture* because these larger systems structure the very way that the world is organized and experienced; they are not simply metaphors or systems of thought, but very complex systems that define and articulate entire ways of living and experiencing and producing meaning. Later I will argue that one goal of the local parish community must be to form a distinctive theological culture through the normal functions of parish activities, but for the moment we should continue to explore culture as a category for analysis of religious experience.

Culture defines the potential, the larger systems upon which humans can call in their lives. Culture becomes concrete at the level of social relationships. Within this broader cultural context, Geertz explains, are "actually existing network of social relations" and "the ongoing process of interactive behavior."[2] Behavior invokes the systems laid out in the culture, that is, the systems present and functioning as options within a given environment, while the culture makes available to an individual all the possible behaviors through stipulating the parameters, direction, and action of social interaction. "Culture is the fabric of meaning in terms of which human beings interpret their experience and guide their action; social structure is the form that action takes."[3] The social structure in our narrative is not difficult to lay out. Mary and I had developed a particular sort of theological relationship emerging from the theological culture in the parish through which we first met as minister and active layperson. Her husband shared this culture to some extent, although not as explicitly as Mary. He could understand the system, but he had insufficient formation in it and experience of it to understand it thoroughly. It had not become so much a part of his life that he could experience the theological culture intuitively. Mary and her family functioned within the normal popular, middle-class culture of her times: her children were married and beginning their own families; most of them had gone to college; the family was closely knit and capable of discussing even difficult matters with clarity and respect for one another even in difference; they were above all deeply committed to one another. They were, in short, a well-functioning family as our society recognizes it, with strong and open communication leading to good relationship. In the absence of her family's theological relationships within the theological culture in which Mary had chosen to live, I had to create experiences that would begin to form social relationships consonant with that theological cultural milieu. This was the function of the Eucharists celebrated with her while she was still alive. These Eucharists replicated in short order and abbreviated time the experience of living in a eucharistically centered community among a diversity of people over a long period of time. Abbreviated to a brief sketch of social relationships not previously envisioned, these Eucharists opened up a new dimension of theological relationship with Mary, a relationship that would become the norm after her death. These Eucharists, in short, initiated the other family members into the theological culture that Mary had chosen and in which Mary lived regularly in her parish life. The local religious community is the only place where such a theological culture, with its attendant nexus of theologically significant

2. Ibid.
3. Ibid.

social relationships, can be developed. In essence, the Eucharist was the instrument of creating a parish within the confines of Mary's family.

Many years earlier, after I left her parish, Mary continued developing her theological relationships by attending various theological-education groups sponsored by various local divinity schools and by her denomination. Her interest in theological formation continued. Mary exhibited a phenomenon that cultural theorists have long understood: the importance of the individual person. Cultural theorists maintain that intersecting both the cultural and the social aspects of life (and often at odds with them) is the individual person, whose personality gathers and activates the potentiality of the various social and cultural systems within which the person operates.[4] Mary could and did choose a theological culture over the medical culture at the end of her life, and she could make that decision because she was sufficiently formed as a person to decide and act within the framework of a different definition of reality than her doctor—and perhaps her family—maintained. Unless she knew, understood, and interiorized these cultural and social systems, she would not have been able to carry them through to action. Admittedly, she was not confident that she had the personal integration sufficient to guide her through the experience, but her theological formation included consultation with people who might assist her in finding God revealed in the midst of her current life situation. My role, however, was strictly confirmation of what she had already known and affirmed. She was capable of functioning in a theological culture by virtue of her reflective and thoughtful living within the culture. She took the Bible seriously, not simply as informer of her own life, but also as the instrument of revelation to the community: that is, Scripture became the locus for discourse in her religious culture so that through it she could learn to see and experience God. Corporate worship became the arena in which her life could find both different social structures (different from the structures of society at large) and a place where reality was defined with the active and immediate presence of God. Through the rituals attending birth, death, grief, forgiveness, daily living, and the seasons of the church year, Mary developed a wide capacity to envision the world and to find meaning for her life within it. The input to this personal development came at every level: the cultural through reading, thinking, reflecting, and studying and through active participation in a community of faith; the social through different relations among the living and a different view of the dead; and the

4. Ibid.

personal through her bringing her own life to add to the lives of the others assembled. Her competence as a religiously cultural participant found its formation in the regular and daily life of a community that gathered to live out its theological culture.

Individuals are involved in multiple cultural and social systems simultaneously, as was Mary and her family. They are capable of either submitting to or fighting against the constraints of these systems. Much of the ability to change or enhance these systems, however, rests on the degree of involvement that the individual experiences. All individuals may be involved in the social and cultural system, but those at the margins of that system will not be implicated in the same way that someone of the dominant class, nationality, or race may be. Those who, like Mary, are most fully involved in the theological milieu of their churches likewise will not be implicated heavily in the culture of the dominant social and cultural system.

It is a dangerous thing to wander into another academic field, and so I will acknowledge that my simple description of anthropological categories reduces the content too much. What is central to my discussion here in this book relates to the suggestive quality of the three major categories that anthropologists explore: culture, social relations, and individuals. These three categories provide us with different lenses through which to view liturgy, spirituality, and corporate spiritual formation.

Culture, Parish, and Public Spirituality

The examples from the life of my former parishioner and her death scene display the complex public nature of religious life. Religious formation does not happen primarily in the individual alone but also occurs in social relationships and in the wider conceptions of the world, life, and death. In the United States we pride ourselves in a separation of church and state, but there has never been, neither here nor throughout history, separation of religion and politics. In recent decades, the American religious Right has made the public aspect of religious formation also a political reality in our common life. Spirituality, however, has been relegated to the private sphere, to a set of practices primarily oriented toward the formation of the religious faith and belief of one person. I maintain that spirituality also is a public activity whose most accessible site for development is the local parish. Although I acknowledge the possibility that a person may be spiritually formed by living in a monastery or in other small religious communities,

I understand the local congregation to be the center for formation for the vast majority of religious people. The local parish is the primary public arena for the exercise of ministry and for the spiritual formation of people.

A definition of *ministry* would help here. Ministry, both of a professional minister and of a layperson, communicates and reveals God by creating an environment in which significant religious revelation and discourse may take place in public. This environment can only be created by communication. Proper communication, in turn, can only take place when some sort of community has been established—community in which communication is enhanced and encouraged by developing a mutual language, by sharing common understandings of word meanings, by imbuing common experience with significance, and by establishing other such systems that develop and define a community in which God may be revealed or communicated. The public nature of religion connects the larger cultural systems to social structures and to personal life, because religion, even if very private, retains its public aspects. Religious community can be created in any public sphere (industry, government, education, medicine) but may most effectively be created in a local parish. At its heart, then, ministry works at creating a religious culture—a culture in which the whole person, the whole society, and every dimension of human existence and history is capable of finding meaning and understanding through the revelation and communication of God.

In the business sector, for example, a corporate culture will develop along very similar patterns without the emphasis, or core of the culture, revolving about the communication of religious revelation or values. When persons enter a corporation, their initial task is not so much to begin doing the job they were hired to do as it is to begin learning the systems that the corporation has developed to communicate its life, to structure the relationships of people within the company, and to regulate the manner of each person's personal integration. Someone who quickly masters the corporate culture is free to begin working effectively and will do well. Someone for whom the corporate culture remains elusive will never communicate well enough to be perceived as performing well, regardless of their actual achievements in their work.

Christian ministry operates in a correlative manner to a corporate culture, but in relationship to the reality of God. Ministry sets out to create a culture that organizes the intellectual, emotional, and personal lives of its people in such a way as to reveal and reflect God's presence. This religious culture takes as its center the reality, presence, and efficacy of God so that the presence of the divine demarcates religious from every other sort of culture. Within this theologically constituted culture, social relations bear a religious significance; that is, in addition to other cultural dimensions of social relations, social interactions in religious culture become revelatory of God. The nature, quality, and structure of these relationships provide a window into the beliefs and understandings of the shared religious culture. In a religious culture, social relations describe theological revelation, and theological revelation can alter the boundaries, structure, and relational options of social relationships within the community. The society at large, for example, might recognize only biological, nuclear families while the religious culture can recognize and help develop other sorts of family groups: for instance, families made up of elders who live together to support one another, same-sex couples, single persons living out their lives together in mutual support and love, or persons unrelated to one another adopting a family structure to create a so-called family of choice. Theological culture can develop and sanction alternative sorts of relationship.

The religious culture formed in ministry develops systems of understanding, formulations, and theologies that give cohesion to living. Although not completely systematic, theological systems will address the primary life experiences so familiar in the ministry such as death, birth, familial relationship, and illness, as well as the primary ways God is revealed in the individual's or society's life, such as through Scripture, sacraments, miraculous gifts, historical tradition, and reason.

People learn the religious culture primarily through living in community with others, through worship and other means of forming corporate experience, and through the interaction of the religious experience with the wider experience in the more multifaceted nonreligious environment. Gradually members of the community are formed; that is, they master the essentials at every level of the theological culture. As members learn to articulate and function in the larger systematic arena, they become capable of evaluating, discerning, and owning their own lives both in social and in cultural dimensions.

The Role of the Minister

At the beginning of this chapter, I described the effect of formation by a member of a religious community in the concrete example my former parishioner, Mary. Now I turn to the role of the minister in the formation of that religious culture. The minister is crucial and central to the development of a religious culture primarily because, as the one who gathers the community and theologically articulates the life of the community, the minister functions as the primary conduit and agent of religious culture. The processes of communication in a culture are very complex (and the next chapter will explore those processes more fully), but let me examine them now through the threefold lens of culture, social structure, and the individual.

First, the minister articulates the larger systems of thought, emotion, and action that structure, inform, and potentially determine the religious life of the society and the individual. These larger systems are not always easy to isolate, but they are operative. Take, for example, information regarding healing. Healing in the medical culture tends to be defined as the restoration of the body to well-functioning wholeness. For the medical community, as the description of a process, *healing* seldom ends in death. For Mary and for the members of our parish, healing also includes the peace that a person who is sick makes with herself, the community, and God—as well as the restoration to fullness of life through death. For the medical community, as the description of a process, *healing* seldom ends in death. The same word, *healing*, invokes both systems in religious thought. The minister begins to articulate the difference between the medical system and the religious system and helps people to function within the religious system. The same would apply, for another example, to the word *justice*. *Justice* in the juridical culture refers to the establishment of right relationship of power and presence as defined by laws and as exercised through a legal system. A person who has been wronged by either another person or an institution seeks justice by bringing a suit in court, and the judge (and sometimes a jury) mediates the redress for the wronged person and inflicts punishment on the wrongdoer. But for religious people, *justice* often refers to the provision for all people through the distribution of power and resources so that even the weak and resourceless people may find provision. The minister articulates these and many other conceptual frames, operative systems such as family, household, relation, privacy, corporate identity, patriotism, life, or death. Every dimension of human existence is transformed in a religious culture. The primary resource for these larger religious and cultural systems rests on various means such as revelation or tradition by which God is understood to be a part of human culture. And the minister is a central agent in this process of revelation.

Second, the minister envisions and describes the development of social relations consonant with the religious culture. The embodiment of the larger systems occurs primarily in the structuring and restructuring of relationships at every level of human existence. The minister assists people to see and to experience different sorts of relationships possible within the cultural milieu. Mary, for example, needed to experience the sort of community in which the living and the dead gather at the Eucharist; although I could have explained it theoretically, somewhere along the line she needed to know in her own experience that she and other members of the community (living and dead) were gathered into one body of baptized people, just as she had rehearsed earlier in our common ministry when we were burying so many elders of the community. Without the embodiment of the theological articulation in actual relationship, Mary could not have become a fully functioning religious person; she could not have become competent to choose the religious culture for the living out of her death. The same applied to her family at the hospital Eucharists; they were guided by the minister into a new relationship, not otherwise envisioned, that enabled them to understand and to give meaning to the death of their mother and wife.

Third, the minister assists individuals in their formation as persons in the religious culture. The minister helps individual people (both personally and through corporate communication) to integrate their religious experience into their way of living through such instruments as well-articulated sermons, pastoral counseling, and outreach ministries. The individual will replicate the cultural and social systems learned within the religious culture by using them as the basis for defining and developing as a full person, and this will provide a corrective to the larger systems when those systems and relationships no longer enable the person to become integrated and religious. The integrative formation of the individual is the part of religious tradition that has been most developed and exploited in the large corpus of literature on individual spirituality that has become so popular in Euro-American culture.

In actuality the minister and the participant in local religious community never work at these three aspects of religious culture separately: the culture is not divorced from social relationships, and neither of these is separate from individual formation. As an agent of religious culture, the minister functions across these three dimensions simultaneously, and the participant in the parish experiences all three simultaneously and without distinction. The minister translates the language and experience of diverse people and groups in the community to other members of the community. This translation makes explicit any number of cultural, social, and individual differences and subgroups within any culture. The minister also explores the underlying significance of common experiences to reveal their theological, religious, and ethical dimensions; to create solidarity in the midst of plurality by laying a common experiential foundation; and to set the meaning and signification of words and concepts for individuals within that particular community. When communication breaks down in the community, the minister connects—or continues to connect—people where there are not other open systems of communication. This communication is partly a matter of translating experience and concerns to others, and partly a means of enabling contrary positions and differences to coexist in community. Finally, the minister encourages the outward and expansive dynamic of community, expanding the community when it has become too much of a closed society, and solidifying the community when it becomes too fluid. Since the culture is a signifying and communicating system, the minister is not at its center, but at every place that transformation and change happens.

It is challenging to think of spiritual formation as the creation of a religious culture enacted primarily through corporate religious activities. Most of the recently published literature on spirituality emphasizes the growth in awareness of the individual alone, seldom exploring the social and corporate dimension to the spiritual life. This is most evident in the proliferation of self-help resources such as books, seminars, webinars, and audio- and videotapes. Self-help has become a major American industry. This exploration of Mary's death has set the stage for moving the conversation about spiritual formation out of the realm of the completely private into the realm of the individual in community. Spirituality is a public and corporate reality that functions within a revelatory culture. That revelatory culture mediates the knowledge and experience of God to people, especially when they gather for liturgical events. Living in a revelatory culture and becoming proficient at living in such a religiously alive environment begins with a process of communication. Spirituality involves the communication of revelation from God to people and from people to society and from society to the individual. Religious people can learn the communicative arts so well that they become a way of life, a mode of living in the world that reflects the centrality of God in life. It is a complex process of communication, involving not only the minister but also all the participants in the parish's life. It is to that complexity of communication to which we now turn.

2

Praying the Bodies

Parish Communication, Liturgy, and Community Spiritual Growth

ON THE EVE OF July 1 in Greece, the beginning of the feast of the dual saints of healing, Cosmas and Damian, who are called the "Holy No-Silver Ones"—*I Agii Anargiri*—because they never asked for payment like the secular healers of their day, the Greek Orthodox community on the island of Paros in the Kyklades gathers at a remote and no-longer-inhabited monastery perched high above the village for a festival evening beginning with vespers, followed by a community supper, and concluding the next morning at sunrise with the celebration of the Eucharist. The little chapel, normally dark and deserted (although always well-kept and clean) is decorated for the occasion: the icons on the walls are garlanded with red and white carnations; embroidered and crocheted white cloths are hung below each large icon to cover the old wood of the icon screen; the brass hanging lamps are cleaned of their year's accumulation of olive oil; the candle stands are cleaned and prepared to receive the beeswax candles of the hundreds of pilgrims who will come for the celebration. At the vespers, the tiny chapel is packed with worshipers. Hundreds of candles illumine the space and make seeing possible. On a small table in the middle of the cramped space stand five enormous loaves of bread (each at least two feet in diameter) that will be blessed during the vespers and distributed to the assembly after the service. The vespers itself begins about 9:30 p.m. (although it is announced for about 8:00 p.m.), and it continues until just about midnight.

Unless you have some understanding of Orthodox religious ethos, this event would remain troublesome, boring, long, and without any apparent logic. However, once the participant learns of the vespers tradition of a feast inaugurating the feast itself, once the participant learns that the blessing of loaves are part of the commemoration of the biblical feeding (of the Israelites in the desert and of the five thousand by Jesus) and are an act of communal thanksgiving to God for sustenance and blessing, and once the participant learns that Greeks normally do not even think about eating their dinner until about midnight, then this festival begins to make sense: it coheres and displays the community's corporate sense of religious identity. Festivals are carefully planned and orchestrated events celebrating the spirituality of the community and fulfilling the prayer needs of the community that understands these events. In the last chapter we discussed a familiar culture as the focus for religious formation; here that religious formation takes place in a decidedly different culture.

I use this sort of foreign cultural frame as a starting point for this chapter. One feels like a tourist at a Greek festival, however, when one attends a parish of a different denomination, or even a different tradition within a denomination, then one does not feel like a tourist. When I was an undergraduate at Hope College in Holland, Michigan, I was still a member of the Greek Orthodox Church. When the Dutch Reformed liturgy began, and someone said, "Let us pray," I immediately stood up, because standing is the proper posture for prayer in the Orthodox Church, but everyone else in the room hunched over with their hands covering their eyes. My embarrassment knew no bounds: even though I was a member of the college and the larger Christian community, I was not a member of the religious culture of the majority of the college members. To a lesser degree, I feel the same cultural displacement when attending a Presbyterian or Methodist liturgy. It is not my own, and I do not know the systems of communication that enable members of that liturgical community to experience it intuitively. And equally, broad- or low-church Episcopalians experience cultural displacement when attending my Anglo-Catholic parishes with their sung liturgies, incense, bowing, making the sign of the cross, and kneeling.

These sorts of experiences have opened new avenues for understanding spirituality for me. Rather than relying on the individual and private aspect of personal and corporate prayer for an understanding of spirituality,[1]

1. This privatized view of spirituality, so consistent with the American ethos (see Bellah, *Habits of the Heart*), has been the focus of most of the modern study of spirituality. The ascendancy of the privatized view of spirituality begins with Pierre Pourrat, who

I have turned to the social and corporate underpinnings of "things of the spirit" to guide my understanding of the term *spirituality*. Spirituality should be understood as an interior system of communication about the experience of faithful living within a cohesive religious community.[2] Let me use my example of the Orthodox vespers to explain this.

I'll use my Greek example for clarity and consistency. Every Greek at the festival vespers at the monastery, and every non-Greek with theological, liturgical, or cultural training understood the systems of communication that were operating; because they understood them, they could readily participate in them during the vespers, the dinner, and its subsequent celebration of the Eucharist. Although probably not consciously aware of the systems, every person present operated with a functional understanding of those systems: at some point each participant learned the proper conduct and sequence of such religious festivals without necessarily knowing or understanding the theology that the festival represents. Tourists, who had no understanding, could not enter into the system, not only because they would not know when and where to go for the celebration, but also because they would not understand what was happening if they did manage to get there. For one to participate in the spirituality of the community, a person needs at least some information or training, but optimally a comprehensive initiation so as to be able to enter into the liturgy and to be fully aware of the meaning of the events surrounding the service. In order to pray, the community understanding and practice of prayer must be known or understood at some operative level. It is my contention that *spirituality* refers to this lived faith as an interiorized system supported by a defined

defined *spirituality* as "that part of theology which deals with Christian perfection and the ways that lead to it" (*Christian Spirituality*, 1:v) and continues with the editors of the *Encyclopedic History of the Religious Quest*, whose working definition of *spirituality* is "that inner dimension of the person called by certain traditions 'the spirit.' This spiritual core is the deepest center of the person. It is here that the person is open to the transcendent dimension; it is here that the person experiences ultimate reality" (quoted in Cousins, ed., *World Spirituality*, xiii). See also Bouyer et al., *History of Christian Spirituality*, vii–xi; and Jones et al., eds., *Study of Spirituality*. My discussion in this chapter, however, will move in a decidedly different direction.

2. My perspective in this book emerges from my attempt to apply critical method to the study of Christian spirituality. Although I do not specifically refer to any theory, the dominant system that I have used is that of Hodge and Kress, *Social Semiotics*, 1–12, who emphasize the interrelated importance of systems of solidarity and systems of modulated power.

community of religious practices, and that prayer, properly understood in its corporate dimension, constitutes the heart of spirituality.

Communication undergirds the social function of spirituality and constitutes the focus of the liturgical assembly. But this communication becomes a complex process because it simultaneously involves individual people and groups of people who participate in a wide variety of communities, cultures, religious traditions, and histories. To embrace so complex a mixing of extended relationships complicates liturgical communication. It is difficult to isolate the various elements and levels at which this communication occurs, even though most people function quite happily in community without consciously knowing the various (mostly nonarticulated) systems supporting them. We, in our search to understand corporate spiritual formation, must learn how to use these systems for corporate spiritual growth.

In this chapter, I propose to introduce a series of distinctions and categories about religious composition that I believe will assist in understanding these systems and their complexities. First, I will present a simple theory of communication and apply it to liturgy. Here the complexity of corporate communication and expression will be highlighted, especially since liturgy becomes the focus of corporate spiritual formation when spirituality itself is defined corporately. Second, I will look at three expressions of the body in the liturgy as a focus of complex spiritual understanding. Three different bodies will be developed as the basis for corporate spiritual formation: the individual body, the social body, and the corporate body. Third, I will problematize the community's spiritual and liturgical life so as to indicate how these various bodies are activated during liturgical prayer and how they affect corporate spiritual formation. And finally, I will extrapolate from these observations to discuss "praying the bodies," that is, praying each one of the bodies as they are here defined.

A Theory of Communication

Let me begin with a very simple theory of communication developed out of a common problem encountered in Christian worship. A few years ago, I preached a stewardship sermon at a parish in which there had been many years of discussion about the redefinition of the meaning of the term *family* to include a very wide variety of possible groupings beyond the traditional biological family grouping. In this sermon, I used the word *family* in suggesting that members of the community extend an invitation to other families to join our community. I explained that since our community's financial support of the parish was very strong, the only way to grow was through increased membership. It was neither a particularly outstanding stewardship sermon nor a particularly unusual analysis of the life of the parish community. A few weeks later, however, I heard about grumbling from some people who described my use of the word *family* as excluding precisely those people we had sought to include as families within the parish. I was characterized as rejecting alternative families in support of only the socially accepted and sanctioned varieties of family—a characterization that did not describe in any way either my public or private opinions and attitudes. The grumbling became hostile. So what went wrong? Why was there such hostility and pain? As it turned out, the people most upset about this situation were members of the community who had great difficulty with their nuclear and biological families and with their parents, especially with abusive fathers. The mere reference to family from a man and from the pulpit—which carried the powerful sanction of the religious institution—stirred up their enormous pain. They were no longer able to hear me, but only to hear the pained response to their own lives stimulated by the circumstances of my speaking a particular word from a particular position of power.

A theory of communication helped me to understand better the processes that took place. Roman Jakobson, a linguistic theorist, has developed a theory of communication that may be outlined in its most reduced form as follows:[3]

Sender → Codes → Receiver

In order for communication to happen, someone must send a coded message to another capable of receiving and understanding the message. This is a complex situation because the sender or giver of the codes must choose from those codes capable of bearing meaning within a given social group in order to insure that the receiver will be able to decode and understand the message. In my example above, I was the sender and I chose codes for my sermon that I thought the entire congregation was capable

3. The theory presented here is from Jakobson, "Closing Statement: Linguistics and Poetics," in Innis, *Semiotics*, 147–75, especially 147–56. Jakobson's theory is significantly more sophisticated than my summary here. For a useful discussion of communication, see also Eco, *Semiotics*, 32–36.

of interpreting and understanding. Within the smaller sphere of my own congregation, I thought I had chosen language about the family that everyone present could hear and understand. The sender cannot communicate meaning idiosyncratically but must choose from those codes available in the social setting in order to make it possible for the receivers to interpret. I thought that the sermon reflected the language and concepts used in preaching throughout my tenure there as a minister. Likewise, the receivers will not understand the message if they choose to define the codes differently than the social setting prescribes, so that my hearers, either through their lack of knowledge about the discourse regarding family or through their own great pain about issues of the family, could not understand the intent or the meaning of the codes that I had sent to them in my reference to the family in my sermon. There was, then, a breakdown in communication. The sender's codes and the codes received were interpreted in reference to two different systems, and, hence, there really was no effective communication accomplished.

This common miscommunication amplifies the difficulty with liturgy and corporate spiritual formation. A simple variation on this system will define this complexity:[4]

Liturgy → Instruments of Communication → Participant

A liturgy is a multifaceted text in the sense that it includes words, gestures, music, costume, movement, and sometimes smell and taste. The liturgy represents an encoded system of messages sent to those who participate in it. In order for these coded systems to communicate, the codes must be so presented that the participant may understand them. This assumes a common context from which both the liturgy and the participant draw, the liturgy for creating the communication and the participant for interpreting the communication. The various elements of the liturgy, encoded with its various means of communication, present the message to the participant, referring to the context that they both understand and that enables the message to make sense.

The same system of liturgical communication also works in reverse:

Participants → Codes → Liturgy

---

4. Hodge and Kress understand "'text' in an extended semiotic sense to refer to a structure of messages or message traces which has a socially ascribed unity" (*Social Semiotics*, 6).

The common matrix of understanding is set by the people who participate in the liturgy and by the social setting in which the liturgy is taking place. By shifting or moving or reassessing codes, the participants can change the meaning of the liturgy, as, for example, when a lesbian couple who has children hears a reference to a biological family and adjusts the meaning mentally to include their variety of family. Codes normally developed in the context of liturgical communication may not be interpreted within the systems in which they were developed. Either participants may not know the system (because they are new to the community or because they were not part of an earlier conversation to which the liturgist refers), or the participants, for whatever reason, may not be able fully to hear or to interpret the liturgical codes.

But liturgy is not a simple system of communication. There is much that is not included. Notice, to begin, that this discussion has avoided the question of the author, or creators, of the liturgy, as well as the question of the leaders or performers of the liturgy. Both of these complicate the theory of communication significantly because the originators of the liturgy and the performers of the liturgy potentially carry divergent and sometimes conflicting significations and levels of understanding to what they are doing. Liturgies, moreover, include many participants who bring a wide variety of cultural systems to bear on the meaning of the codes: these differences may represent social, racial, class, theological, ethnic, psychological, or sexual systems among many other possibilities.[5] The larger the group, the less specific the content of the coded message can be—there is a wide spectrum of possible and potential interpretations that follow from group involvement.

In my illustration above about my sermon, there were a number of different points at which communication did not happen. The preacher and the individual listeners to the sermon each had complex histories, psychologies, levels of education, abilities and gifts, and pains that determined the manner of their performance. The preacher and the listeners had social relations both within the community and outside it—social relations that supported the preacher in advocating the growth of the parish through invitations to other families, and that simultaneously supported the disgruntled listeners to interpret the statement as exclusive and withholding.

---

5. These divergent and complex potentialities are documented thoroughly in Hodge and Kress, *Social Semiotics*, 37–38. The context itself carries meaning as well as the participants in any process of communication.

And finally, there was a corporate entity involved in that the preaching took place in a corporate setting in which the community had developed a conversation about the meaning of family.

This complex system of liturgical communication may be analyzed further by distinguishing the various forms of participation made possible by liturgical assembly. What emerge as central to our understanding are three foci to our communication system on each side of the codes: an individual, social, and corporate body of the sender of the codes; and an individual, social, and corporate body of the receiver of the codes. These three bodies (individual, social, and corporate) deserve some discussion.

The Three Bodies

Basic to this essay is a sort of religious anthropology whose primary categories are the individual body, the social body, and the corporate body.[6] The body is the individual person, an identity and recognizable personality limited and denoted by the physical body that includes all the functions, which we recognize from the perspective of our experience of ourselves: it would comprise any number of metaphoric systems, including medical, psychological, traditional spiritual, and common folk traditions, among a wide assortment of metaphors.[7] The social body is the internal community, which is developed by each individual in relationship to other people and to the wider social environment; that is, it is the body in relationship to the outer environment, both human and natural.[8] This is the body that becomes part of a wide nexus of social relationships with individual people (parents, siblings, grandparents, aunts and uncles, school friends, mentors, idols, among many others) and social relationships emergent from

6. This religious anthropology has been the subject of much of my research in asceticism over the past few years. See Valantasis, "Daemons," 47–79; and Valantasis, "Constructions of Power in Asceticism," 775–821; the particular application of historical-theological research about the practice of spirituality encourages the integration of academic work and parish ministry. This was presented more theoretically in Valantasis, "An Essay on Ministry and Culture," 334–45.

7. I am particularly indebted for my understanding of the body to two sources: Lakoff and Johnson, *Metaphors We Live By*; and Haraway, "The Biopolitics of Postmodern Bodies."

8. Anthropologists and related theorists have helped form this concept, which has been widely discussed in a variety of disciplines. Here I am particularly indebted to the work of Douglas, *Purity and Danger*; and Malina, "Pain, Power, and Personhood."

the social environment (church associations, cultural organizations, sports teams, ethnic assemblies, among others). Both the internal and the external social relationships develop the person as a social body. The corporate body is the conglomeration of all the bodies in cultural movements. This corporate body gathers up all the individual bodies together with their social bodies into larger functioning cultural constructions. The corporate body is the body strictly defined from the social perspective of the conglomeration of social entities in larger social association.[9] The anthropological distinctions, then, are the body and its functions, the body in its interior social community, and all bodies as a group. This differentiation of kinds of body (individual, social, and corporate) will assist us to understand the process of corporate spiritual formation.

In order for spiritual growth to occur, each one of these aspects of human existence must be addressed. Spirituality, as a system of communication about the interior life of a community, cannot operate simply at the level of the individual, because then it would not be communicable or interpretable; nor can it simply operate socially, because then it would not change the individual or the corporate culture in which an individual functions; nor can it simply be corporate, because then both the individual and the social aspects of human existence would neither support it nor enable it to thrive. The full human being, in every aspect of its human development and relatedness, must be the heart of spiritual growth and the development of spirituality. The same applies to prayer: if it is to embrace the totality of one's existence, prayer must incorporate all three bodies. Let me explore these three aspects of human development further, with reference to a particular and very significant event in our parish life.

The Individual Body

Little Peter was conceived and nurtured in our parish. His parents were both active members and were interconnected to every part of the parish community, including choir, vestry, church school, social justice and mission, recycling, stewardship, building maintenance, children's pageants, liturgy, lectoring, and just about every other task in the parish that needed to happen. Their first child, a daughter, was practically a member of every

---

9. Again, I am indebted to many theorists for the development of this concept, especially to the kind of rhetorical, semiotic, and cultural analysis of Roland Barthes: see Barthes, *Mythologies*; and Barthes, *The Rustle of Language*.

other family in the parish, and their second child quickly became a parish child as well. We knew him, and loved him, even before he was born, as we prayed over his mother, father, and sister throughout the pregnancy.

As a very young baby, Peter was diagnosed with leukemia. Our child was seriously ill, and the whole parish galvanized to help him and his family deal with the stress of hospital and home, school and work. We became part of his extended family, staying with him through the night so that the parents could stay home with their daughter, waiting with his parents for news from tests and other doctors' reports. Peter entered a remission after his initial serious bout. We all thought we had experienced a miracle. Our son was better now.

After a few years, Peter's leukemia began anew. We were devastated, and we followed the ups and downs of his little body throughout its cycles: we all ached with it, we all felt its weakness, we all experienced his frustration and loneliness when he was in isolation following his bone-marrow transplant. When Peter was at church, we would all gather around him after the liturgy to lay hands on him, to anoint him, and to pray for his recovery. It was (as we were to learn) a losing battle. The transplant only worked long enough for us triumphantly to welcome him back to our liturgical assembly with balloons, applause, and a tearful welcome home. The very next week, he began his serious decline, and very shortly thereafter he was released from the hospital to spend his last days at home.

The co-rector of the parish and I received word that Peter was dying, but by the time we arrived, Peter, still in his Ninja turtle pajamas, had just died in his parents' arms; the family and friends were still in shock. Since it was late, his parents decided to keep him at home for the night. The co-rector and I called the undertaker to come early in the morning, and then we helped parents and friends to wash his body, to wrap him in a sheet as in a shroud, and to watch with him in a vigil. During the vigil before his shrouded body, we prayed, recited psalms, cried, hugged one another, and looked on the rested face of a child who had fought vigorously for his life.

Peter's body, as the doctors knew it, was the scientific body, the one marked by his leukemia and the one they attempted through many medical means to save. The scientific, medical body functions as an individual, a complex set of functions bounded by the form of the body. Peter's body was that before which we kept vigil and that which we wrapped in a sheet in its death, after all of the systems that could support physical life had ceased to function. Generally in American culture, to understand the way a human being lives is to posit an isolated, discrete person. The person is scientifically defined as a system that operates in its own body. This body lives a particular lifestyle determined by race, class, gender, and resources. This body moves in and out of various relationships but remains essentially the same throughout all this activity. This is a very static view of what it means to be a human being (a view that is very privatized) that most of us accept because we have accepted the various medical metaphors and ideologies presented to us in our American culture.

The Social Body

After the evening vigil with Peter in his home, the undertaker came to take his body and to prepare it for burial. It was our custom in that parish to bring the body into the Blessed Sacrament Chapel for visitation by family and friends: our community theology embraced the fact that the Body of Christ in the sacrament would mirror the body of the Christian in eternal life. Hundreds of people came to the visiting hours, forming an interconnection with him that extended from his grade-school class to people who had long ago moved away from the parish: friends, relatives, family, parishioners of long association with Peter, parishioners who met him first in one of the many hours spent with him at the hospital, parishioners who had not known him in his living body but would be part of the all-night vigil before the closed casket in the church. The concept of the *dead* body did not account for what people were feeling in relationship to Peter and to each other. Some other kind of association was coming into existence and was being celebrated in these events: Peter's body was not only identified with the medically defined body in the casket but also with the interconnections of his life with those at the church that evening and with the interconnections created through his living and dying among the people who had gathered. These interconnections I call the *social body*.

The social body of the person describes the wide assortment of people who have become a part of our lives, who live with us in our bodies, because they are biological family or family of choice, friends, compatriots in a political party, members of a religious community, people in the same place in their lives, or working associates. The list can continue. There are for each of us, as part of our mode of living, people who have become virtually a part of us, a part of the fabric of our lives, a part of our interiorized social body. Surely the religious community is a part of us, as are people who have died (grandparents, aunts and uncles, close friends, lovers), to name just a few possibilities. The social body (that is, the body implicated in a wide spectrum of social relationships past and present) cannot be defined simply as that one body determined by the physical body.

The social body is further developed at the worship space. Here the social body relates not just to immediate social bonds but also to historical social relationships, to the impersonal inherited religious tradition, to the deceased who are claimed as part of the social body both personally and institutionally, and to the members of one's social body who have died or who are distant, who are connected through worship to the space and time in which worship occurs. There are other inhabitants in the pews than those whose scientific bodies are visible.

The Corporate Body

The perspective on these two bodies must shift for an examination of the corporate body, because the corporate body views the assembly of individual and social bodies as a unified body made up of many parts (individual and social bodies) but functioning cohesively. This will become clearer in looking again at the parish's life after Peter's funeral.

Forty days after Peter's death, the family and community gathered for a memorial service. Bread was baked communally the day before the Sunday service by representatives of parts of Peter's social body: by his family, schoolmates, friends, clergy, godparents, and others who were grieving. The bread was brought into the church as a representation of Peter's being brought again to the church, and as a thank-offering from the community for Peter's life. After prayers (taken from the Burial Office that in turn were taken from the Orthodox *Trisagion*), the bread was distributed to the assembled family and friends, and to all the other members of the worshiping community that day, whether they knew Peter or not.

The service addressed the need of the corporate body of which Peter had become an important part. The corporate body is the conglomeration of all the bodies in a social relationship—the body no longer defined from its individual perspective but from the perspective of all bodies socially related. The corporate body is the body made up by the unity of all the individual and social bodies gathered together into one aggregate, one body. Peter, whether or not members of the congregation knew him in his body, had become a part of the corporate body. His presence was articulated not as an individual, but as part of the history of the community that had a formative impact on the religious development of others in the community, but whose memory, as part of the corporate memory, continued to be present in the community. The corporate body describes the body of all those present in the community, those understood as members of a larger body whose contours cannot be understood or comprehended only as the number of people physically present in the community. Peter, then, joined the list of other deceased members of the parish: the woman in the wheelchair who was so important to many; the monk who was priest-in-charge of the parish for many years when it was still a monastic mission parish; the monks whose photographs hung on the wall of the Common Room, whose names were disputed by current members, but who were nonetheless a vital part of the missionary identity of the parish.

These deceased members form a major part of the corporate body of the parish, but there are many others. The corporate body also extends to all those active and inactive members who have involved themselves in the life of the parish, to those who have come to the parish in time of need, to those poor who come daily for sandwiches, to those who come weekly to our community supper for the homeless and indigent, to those who have casually passed through. And then, of course, there are those who are regular attenders at the Sunday liturgy, and all who are a part of the social body of each person there come with him or her into the corporate body. The corporate body is a widely divergent and complex assembly of persons whose lives collect together to become a being in itself.

The differentiation of these three bodies undergirds our understanding of both the complexity of parish communication and the complexity of Christian prayer. For parish communication, the three bodies problematize very simple realities: Who is actually speaking? What are the permeable boundaries within a cohesive community? What (and whose) language and meanings are to be used in the corporate setting? What language and experience has the community developed? What communication is appropriate to each one of the bodies? This complexity challenges rather than inhibits parish communication. The challenge applies as well to prayer: Which of the bodies is dominant in prayer? Who is the praying subject? To whom is prayer addressed and by whom? How do the bodies relate in prayer? What is prayer in the complex nexus of permeable boundaries in the bodies? Communication (both personal and corporate) and prayer are linked in the interaction of the three bodies.

The Three Bodies Problematized

The way these various bodies interact in a community reveals both the complexity with which communication occurs in a communal setting and the complexity of spiritual formation that must build on that communication. Another incident might illustrate this.

One Lent a few years ago, our parish prepared two candidates for baptism—an woman and a little girl about two and a half years old. Both candidates had been eager for baptism, expressing their eagerness in ways particular to each and appropriate to their respective ages. The young girl had been eager to receive communion with her family and her brothers and especially with the other little children in her church-school class. She eagerly came forward for the prayers over the baptismal candidates throughout Lent, and she was excited about her own baptism at the rehearsal the week before Holy Week. On Easter Eve at the Great Vigil of Easter, she came to church dressed in a white hat, white gloves, and a polka-dot pinafore, and carrying a white purse. She loved her new clothes, and she was very excited, even though the service was beginning long after her regular sleeping time. She fidgeted throughout the service, getting more and more tired so that her father took her out of the service a few times simply to try to help her unwind. When the time for the baptisms came, she came forward in the procession to the baptismal font and was having a relatively nice time of it until it came time for her to take off her new hat, gloves, and purse in order to be baptized. When her hat and purse were being taken from her, she began to scream, "No, I don't want to!" Soon, however, she was in the baptismal waters, still not very happy, but fully immersed and fully chrismated and then clothed in her special white clothing. She seemed fine to all those in the immediate presence of the baptismal font.

That evening at the parish supper and over the next few days, a number of parishioners complained that the child was baptized against her will; that when she cried out no, it was a violent act against her, and that we should have stopped the service. Some people, fearful that her baptism would be remembered as a traumatic religious event, were concerned that her baptism would in fact permanently damage the young girl's religious formation.

However, the day after her baptism, at the solemn Eucharist of Easter Day, which is normally a special service for the children (including a children's sermon and Easter Egg hunt in the sanctuary), the young girl was thrilled to receive her first Communion with her family and with all the other children who were her friends. After the service, she wanted especially to play in the baptismal font, the place where, as she put it, "I took my special bath." The traumatic crying of the evening before seemed not to hold any weight with her now.

Our parish had a large number of people who had been abused in their childhood, and a large number of people who had emerged from very conservative religious families in which they experienced religious coercion: most had spent years in psychological therapy to overcome the trauma of their experiences. When the child cried out, the social bodies of these parishioners were activated: their experience of abuse in their families, in their childhood religious life, and in their marriages became the issue focused on this little child. The fact that the child was naked for baptism invoked the many images of childhood sexual abuse. The fact that the child seemed to have been rejecting baptism (even though we who were nearby knew that she was upset at giving up her new clothes), and that we proceeded to baptize her invoked the religious traumas of many people of the parish. Her little body, presented for baptism, became the focus of activation for a wide variety of social-body realities of parish members.

But this is not to say that because this child's baptism activated many personal experiences of members of the community, that this was entirely a personal problem for those members of the parish. Our corporate body had been built upon the varied experiences of the congregation, and through the extensive discussion of these various experiences in community meetings, sermons, forum discussions, and pastoral relationships. A major part of our corporate body's identity revolved around intense experience of rejection, abuse, and religious trauma. Those experiences, even though not directly the life experience of everyone, became the life experience of everyone in the community by virtue of its presence in one person, and by virtue of our community's open discussion of such traumatic experiences. The corporate body develops its personality precisely through just such experiences. Talking through such issues as this baptism and what happened enabled the community to recognize the issues and contours of its own corporate personality. Simply to explain the confusion at the time of baptism would not have calmed the fears and concerns of the community: the events of the baptism needed to be discussed fully because the issues raised by the child's being upset at her baptism were not focused on the child alone. Nor was the concern over the child's being upset only a problem of a few members of the community; it was a point of clarification of the corporate body of the parish. By discussing such painful issues and the joys and hurts behind the concern over this child's baptism, the parish came to understand who it was, who were its members, and whose experience the members of the community shared.

Praying the Bodies

The interrelationship of these three types of body, the personal, the social, and the corporate, provides a basis for understanding spiritual formation. The growth and development of the individual cannot be sustained without a commensurate growth in the social body (the nexus of relationships that can sustain a person in living) and without a commensurate growth in the corporate body (the community of people who enable the person to live cohesively in the chosen spiritual life). The process for this corporate spiritual formation is one I call *praying the bodies*. In this context, prayer may no longer be understood as the privatized communication of an individual with a distant God but as a process of gathering one's bodies in communion not only with God but with all those who also commune with God. Prayer is a corporate process. Prayer leads to spiritual development as each body takes on its own distinctive form of communion with God.

Prayer is the mutual communication between God and humans. As the primary process of spiritual formation, *praying the bodies* defines the complex communion that takes place not only in the bodies but also with God. Prayer begins in the corporate body and eventually extends to each of the other bodies—first the social and only then to the individual. Prayer originates in the corporate body precisely in the sort of corporate communication that calls together all the bodies into communication with God. The Christian begins to pray at the liturgy, in the corporate body, when the full Body of Christ is present and engaged. The experience of having the wounds of each social body opened to corporate healing and prayer, as in the community's experience of the young girl's baptism, becomes an intense and intentional focus of activity in the corporate body. This corporate body ultimately is the Body of Christ: the Body to which each one was joined at baptism, the Body to which everyone who has ever been baptized has been joined, the Body that will continue until the end of time. Prayer begins, then, with the activation of the corporate baptismal reality that is the foundation of all other human identity and activity, because no individual may leave aside the correlative social or corporate bodies. When the

Christian speaks within the Body of Christ, the Christian begins to pray through song, movement, words, gestures, listening, speaking: initiating and responding within the company of praying bodies that includes all participants who have entered into communion with God. The finite capacities of the individual and social bodies no longer limit the capacity of the corporate body for transformation and renewal. The company of praying people includes automatically the myriad of Christians and other faithful people throughout the ages, the immediate community and all its forebears, and the social bodies of the people present at the liturgy. True prayer for the Christian involves simply communicating within the Body of Christ, especially as that body gathers up all the people of God into one Body of God. Learning to live and to communicate in the Body of Christ, the parish—the corporate Body—becomes the primary manifestation of Christian prayer. Liturgy, especially at the chief worship on Sunday, provides the primary training ground for Christian spiritual formation because it is the primary place where the corporate Body of Christ is manifest and operative.

As one lives in the corporate Body (now I will capitalize the word *Body* to encourage the ambiguity) and becomes transformed in the baptismal life, the social body begins to develop and grow as well. This happens in two arenas: my own personal social body, and the social body constructed of the many relationships formed in the corporate Body. My social body becomes aware of the transformative connection with the corporate Body so that what is broken and fallen in my relationships may be opened to healing and what is strong and good in my relationships are encouraged and renewed. This is effected through prayer. In my praying with others (and even the term *prayer* now is ambiguous), even if I have not experienced the same traumatic or felicitous life events of those surrounding me, I enter into their trauma or grace through the social body. By participating in the Body, I am capable of becoming part of a wider experience, and to make that experience my own. At the same time, that which is happening within is also happening without: people who are part of the corporate Body also become a part of my social body through friendship, through mutual ministry, or merely through participation in the same liturgy. My social body expands not only to include those with whom I have lived, who live within me, but also to include those who have become a part of me because of my participation in the corporate Body. As was the case with little Peter, even people who did not know him in the body could include him in their social bodies, and those of us who had an intense relationship with

31

him could continue to live with him present in our social bodies. These relationships also enter my communion with God. My prayer, then, speaks from a widely interconnected series of relationships far beyond the limits of my own life, and extending far back into the history of the people of God.

Only within this corporate context does individual and private prayer make sense. Even when praying alone, the Christian is not really alone. As a member of the corporate Body, and as one whose social body consists of both the living and the dead, the present and the absent, the Christian recognizes that private prayer is simply a prayer spoken when an individual body finds itself isolated physically from others. When I cannot physically be present with the corporate Body, and when I cannot relate to my exterior social body, I stand in my individual body, carrying the other bodies into my prayer, into my communication with God, into my communion—and I pray the bodies, I speak to God with all the bodies gathered. The true prayer of the corporate Body sustains the individual body in its isolation; the wider connections of the social body sustain the individual body in its separation. The hope, and the reality, however, always is to live as a part of the corporate Body. The aim is toward true prayer in the Body of Christ that my physical isolation denies me temporarily.

Praying the bodies simply becomes the primary activity of those who are baptized members of the Body of Christ. Although I should say that even though I do not have immediate experience to prove the point, I suspect that other religions, faiths, and spiritual communities have a deep sense of the corporate body and its importance to the spiritual life. The Christian systems of communication, made known in the liturgy and through the various bodies, ultimately become systems of prayer, of communion, of faithful living. Living in the Body of Christ over many years, the participants become adept at the sort of communication, which happens through the bodies, and they become adept at a prayer that gathers up every aspect of living in communion with God. Over the years, we begin to recognize each other's social and individual bodies as together we become a corporate Body. This recognition constitutes an interior system of communication, like the one present in the vespers of Cosmas and Damian in Paros: we can see it in one another (as they did), we can understand it about each other, we can experience it together over and over again because it has become a real bond of communion. It is that bond of communion that links Peter's life to my life forever, and that makes the painful reality of sexual abuse experienced by members of my corporate Body a part of my own reality and life. It is that bond of communion that links my prayer with the prayer of all God's people everywhere, in every time and era. It is that bond of communion that is an interior system of communication about the experience of faithful living within a cohesive religious community, the Body of Christ, which at once defines spirituality and models *praying the bodies*.

3

The "Language of Angels"

Narrative, Language, and the Culture of Prayer

EVERY PARISH HAS A story to tell. That story, developed through retelling, describes for people the constituent parts of the life of the community by explaining the terms of membership, the quality of relationships within the community, the values held by members of the community, the conflicts that face the community, and the history of those conflicts. The community narrative communicates a great deal of information about the people, the place, and the events that shaped and molded the community. Above all, however, the recitation and continual development of the parish narrative creates a common language among the participants in the community for contextualizing their own experience of the community and for participation in it.

Let me outline one community narrative from my own past experience as a starting point for discussing the formation of a corporate language. Our parish in Boston was an Anglo-Catholic community. It was founded by a group of Anglican monks, the Society of St. John the Evangelist, known popularly as the Cowley Fathers, and it was a center of missionary activity in the Anglo-Catholic tradition. Actually the Cowley Fathers established two Catholic parishes: one for the rich of Beacon Hill and the elegant of Boston, and one for the poor and the disenfranchised. Ours was the poor parish, and we embraced the poverty and the relationship with the common people. Our parish was on the back side of Beacon Hill; we were on the edge of Scully Square, the combat zone of the city near Boston Harbor known in colonial American times as Whore's Hill, and the building was located on the part of the hill where the servants to the rich lived in cheap housing. That inexpensive housing also attracted houses of prostitution, rooming houses for the working poor, and the poor on the edge of losing what little housing they had. We were definitely not the elegant part of Boston!

As gentrification took hold, our part of town became elegant, and Scully Square was torn down to be remade into a modern and upgraded government center: the part of town where all the courthouses, city government buildings, and state offices were located. Our parish continued to serve the poor, especially those displaced by the redevelopment of the area, by providing regular, daily food programs, evening hot meals, clean clothes, and whatever social services we were capable of providing, either through scraping up enough money to hire someone or (more commonly) through volunteers from the parish.

Our story began with our spiritual origins in a minority theology in the Episcopal Church and developed through stories about the "old days" when we were the major church for the poor and disenfranchised in the city proper. We knew the names of the older generation of monks and priests who served the parish, who were known among the both male and female prostitutes in Scully Square, the recipients of the monks' first missionary zeal. We knew the stories of preaching missions, feeding programs, processions of the Blessed Sacrament, and the assembly of people who did not count to many others, and it became our story.

We added to that narrative by attaching our stories about the inclusion of gay, lesbian, bisexual, and transgendered people whom society (and unfortunately even the church) more and more despised. We added stories about the mission to people who had turned away from Christianity years before out of a sense of the church's abusive and narrow-minded stances with regard to a whole range of social and personal issues, and we also added the stories of their gradual entrance into Christianity to consider anew their Christian faith. We told the stories of being a close-knit community for whom every person was important. We added the stories of those whom we loved who had died and whom we buried in our parish memorial garden; we added the stories of struggles with bishops over the realities of living with gay and lesbian families; we added the stories of the many saints who had valiantly lived out their Christian lives despite enormous pain and sacrifice on the edge of proper Boston society. We were telling the story of the angels both ancient and modern who lived among us, who gathered to fill in the space in which we worshiped, and who were so vital a part of our common life, even for people who had never even heard the full story of their accomplishments and gifts. Our narrative as a parish developed for us a language of angels that enabled us to live out our prophetic life and that empowered us to be a new kind of people. And that narrative will never end: in each event of the parish's life, the story continues to be developed.

Our parish's narrative described for us, often in vivid detail, what it meant to be members of that community. It embodied our values of loyalty and faithfulness to the poor and disenfranchised. It rehearsed our deep commitment to include the financially poor and the socially marginalized in our community. It told newer members about the people that mattered most to us who have died and gone before, but whose presence is still known and felt. The narrative was the first step in developing a common language for us all—a formative language that both guided and supported us in living a prophetic life.

The development of a community narrative represents a major component in the corporate spiritual formation of a community. The narrative points to a language system peculiar to a community. By this particular language system, I simply mean that particular words are invested with a corporate meaning that derives from the life of a particular community alone. For example, the term *burial of the dead* will continue to have its normal generic referent or denotative meaning, while at the same time bearing the specific referent to those members of the community who have died, the experiences of death and burial in our particular community. The term will bear both a common, denotative meaning and a specific set of community meanings or connotations. For our community, the *burial of the dead* invoked older images of monastic funerals, of burials of the anonymous poor by the monastic priests and later by the parochial clergy, and of provision for widows and children orphaned by the death of their financial supporter. The corporate language attains an increment of depth and becomes rich in its specificity within the community, as it develops specific community connotations. The development of a language peculiar to a community makes communication expansive and easier: expansive in that the referents to the language become polysemic, multireferential, and specific; easier in that the rich depth of linguistic usage becomes immediately present.

This narrative function correlates to the various ways bodies may be understood as individually, socially, and corporately situated. Here the parish narrative, from its beginnings to the present, functions as a kind of individual body. It constitutes the particularity of this parish as distinct from all others. To that individual body, our parish added stories that elaborated and expanded its social body by adding generation after generation of stories about that individual body. Not only did our forebears in the faith at that parish minister to the disenfranchised of their day, but we also continued to add stories from our own days of ministering to the disenfranchised. As these various social bodies gathered over a number of years and built the congregation, we developed the corporate body of our parish. This corporate body encapsulated all of the worshiping congregations that had ever been part of this parish throughout its history, and connected those congregations throughout the history of the faith that ministered to the poor, the despised, and the marginalized.

But it was much more than that. The spiritual body, the parish as a real and vitally functioning Body of Christ, developed a particular kind of theology relating to the identification with the poor and rejected, to our engagement in their lives, and to their being welcomed into ours. As a Body of Christ, we developed a particular ministry, vocation, and identity that enabled us all not only to continue the narrative of our parish's life but to develop and expand the core ministry that lay at the heart of the parish's life. The narrative bodies enabled us to continue to develop a narrative spirituality organized around the particularities of our common life.

This narrative assisted us in developing a particular language, a dialect of Christian speaking, that related to a specific and concrete identity of a parish. The narrative enabled us to attach meaning and deeper signification to the words used to articulate our common life. *The poor* for us were not only specific people who came to our feeding programs and who also came to our liturgies during our feast days. *The poor* reached back to innumerable people disenfranchised or rejected by the larger society back at the very beginning of our parish: the prostitutes of Scully Square, the servants from Whore's Hill who worked for the rich on the other side of Beacon Hill, the newly urban deinstitutionalized, the gay and lesbian folks who found their way to our door. The same could be said about the words *family* and *household* and *believer* and *seeker* and *community* and *mission*, and all the other words that we used regularly to articulate to one another and to God our particular vocation in the church and our mission to society.

In most parishes, this common language develops without any intentional activity. It is a common feature of human socializing that social groups of people develop peculiar language patterns. In spiritual formation, however, this common language must be articulated as an intentional aspect of spiritual formation. I would like to explore a few of the ways this language may develop and infuse liturgy with deep and rich meaning. I will discuss language formation in three dimensions: in the pastoral relationship with an individual person (using the analogy of the individual body), in intentional corporate activity that will illustrate the development of language in the social body, and in a model of sermon preparation that will explore language development in the corporate body. The rich language of the corporate body develops out of a community's response to situations, events, problems, and joys within the community, and the language becomes infused with the response to these events. But the language also develops in relation to the vision or goal for community living so that the language reflects the newly imaged realities of Christian living. In this chapter, the development of language will be explored in its pastoral, social, and corporate dimensions. The corporate dimensions will be explored through a program for the development of theological language, through sermons as a language creator, and through the exploration of styles of denominational language.

Individual Language Development

A few years back, a young man in his twenties who had just buried his partner who had died of AIDS was himself hospitalized with an ailment that indicated that he too was dying of AIDS. While nursing his partner through his long illness, this young man did not want to know whether he too was infected with the virus, so that all of his attention could be focused on nursing the man he loved. Very soon after his partner's death, however, the young man found himself in the same hospital room, at the same hospital, with the same medical personnel, with the same symptoms that began his partner's long ordeal. This happened within a few months of his partner's burial.

When I went in to see him at the hospital, the young man was clearly very depressed. He did not want to try to live. He did not want anyone else to go through what he had gone through in nursing his partner. He saw no reason to begin medication or to eat in order to sustain himself or even to cooperate with the doctors. He simply wanted to die and to end the ordeal as quickly as possible. Grief over his partner and grief over his own life mingled and confused his reactions so that all of his life was overclouded and dark.

The young man and I began a process of talking to each other about things that most young men never consider important, and that most people do not ever face, even when they are old. Our conversation revolved about the meaning of life, the sanctity of a full life, the boundaries over which a sick person does not want to pass, the grief over the pain endured in nursing someone only to have them die painfully, the differentiation of his life and sickness from his partner's even when those illnesses were taking a strikingly similar direction. Our conversation embraced the meaning of a godly life in his circumstances, the significance of living in the Body of Christ, the guarantee of immortal life promised us in the gospel, the joy of life after death, the mystery of life in the mystical Body of Christ and in the heavenly chorus that gathers in the Eucharist, the poignancy of life lived in the memory of those still living and still working for the reign of God, and the comfort of the communion of saints lived among the others who have died and gone before and who rest eternally in our parish's memorial garden. Our conversations, infused as they were by the immediacy of life-and-death decision making, created the bond that enabled this young man to re-vision his life, to imagine a different way of living with his dreadful illness.

Eventually, after many weeks of daily conversations and of meeting with friends, family, and colleagues, the young man was released from the hospital to begin treatment and to enter a protocol for research on AIDS. The language of imagining his illness in the context of a deep personal faith lived out in the context of a group of people who also believed and supported his belief made it possible for him to embrace his illness, his life, and his death with a deep and abiding confidence in God. That confidence, articulated through the appropriation of theological language, gave both of us life. Our commitment to one another was that I would be there when he died, and that I would help him to enter the new life about which we talked, and that I would help create the discourse of life that we had begun in his illness with those who survived him in his death.

Over those months in the hospital (and then the few years following), we created a particular means of communication about important issues and we enhanced a parish discourse about death and dying. The new language was a language began to help him sort out the difference between his partner's illness and his own, and to help him make sense of his own life before God and in the presence of the community of the faithful. The enhanced community language revolved about the remembrance and focus on the death of his partner and the preaching and praying that went on around that event, the memorial service to close the official forty-day period of mourning, and the death (both from AIDS and from other illnesses) and burial of so many other people in the parish. The pastoral language between us both guided the corporate language that had already been developed and flowed from that corporate language.

The language referred to two specific times: first, it pointed to the time that the young man would be released from the hospital to begin his own chronic adjustment; second, it pointed to the time of his own death when there would not be time or energy for many words or ideas, but when we would need to invoke the images and the content of these earlier conversations in gesture, touch, and mere reference. In other words, the language functioned to empower his living, to give rich depth and direction to his life even though the length of his life was now severely limited. At the same time, the language became a sort of shorthand of reference that had rich meaning, but which could evoke larger conversations and meanings only through the reference.

We talked, for example, of death as a process of being birthed into another dimension of life in Christ, and that, like birth, there really was no way either to prevent it once it had begun to happen, or to prevent it from happening at all. Once the birthing process begins, we endure and rest in it until it is completed, until the new life begins. This metaphor helped the young man to recognize that his illness was just the beginning of a period of life-giving gestation for him, and that this gestation would take a long time and with proper help and attention would bring rich potential for full and wonderful living. At the same time, the metaphor also prepared the way for the time of his dying to be understood as the final agony of labor and the beginning of a new life. The metaphor, while he was healthy, enabled him to live. The metaphor, when he was very sick and dying, enabled him to enter into the experience of his own death with an understanding of its place in his life. In his weakened state, we needed only refer to his birth pangs and he recalled the whole conversation in its richest dimension.

The development of such a language cannot happen quickly. It takes time to develop the metaphors, to discover the right words, to invoke the proper theological categories, and to enflesh that language with the particular experience of the individual and of the community. It takes time to use common words and to attach other connotative meanings based in the life experience of an individual person. Most of the time, ministers and church people operate with a kind of strictly denotative language, a language based on the simplest dictionary meaning of words. To those denotative meanings, however, each member of a community must begin to attach connotations that arise from within their life experience. That attachment begins when individuals come to a point where their language becomes central to their survival and to their thriving as religious people. In the case of my young parishioner with AIDS, his survival depended on shifting the meaning of words by reorienting them away from one life situation (the death of his lover) and toward another (his own illness).

That same process constructing meaning around critical and important issues could be seen among many others in the parish. The gay and lesbian families in the parish redefined the word *family* through adjoining expansive connotative situations. It was not just that the word *family* referred to gay and lesbian households but that the specifics of their struggles were included: the specific couples and their stories of creating a family, the struggle to adopt or to have children, the frequent conflict with biological families about their way of living, the common need to be circumspect in the workplace about their sexuality and family arrangements. The connotations of the words developed rich depth precisely because of the specificity of referent in the lives of people present in the community. As each member faced similar needs to form and articulate new ways of living, the common language of the parish developed.

The development of the language of a corporate body (whether of two people or a hundred people) requires that the effort and the task begin early and persist through every sort of experience a person or a corporate body confronts. This language both directs the community's experience and grows out of it, but it always enhances the communication necessary to relate with speed and ease and with theological integrity and richness.

The Corporate Development of Language

The same process of development happens in the communal setting and can be developed through liturgy. Let me give another example to illustrate the process.

A few years ago in the parish we suffered the death of four of our members in quick succession. It was a very difficult year—one which none of us will ever forget. It started just before Christmas, in late November, when one parishioner, a young man diagnosed with AIDS, became sick with what appeared to be manageable infections and their complications. He told people at the Sunday coffee hour that with new treatment protocols it would be a long time before the disease killed him. He died unexpectedly and very suddenly that very week. We had his funeral before the next Sunday. The community was not prepared; nor were those who had been his primary support. It was a difficult funeral.

Borrowing from monastic tradition of burial embedded in our parochial identity, we began with Brian, the deceased man's partner, to put together a liturgical cycle for the funeral that would help us to mourn and grieve our members at their death. The liturgies included receiving the body at the church, according to the Episcopal Prayer Book; keeping visiting hours at the church in the Blessed Sacrament chapel; observing a ceremonial closing of the casket after visiting hours; and singing Compline, a vigil with the body through the night, during which members of the congregation recited the Psalter; and observing the solemn Funeral Mass the next day. It was a system that worked well, I think, in that it provided sufficient time with the body to recognize the death of the person, while locating that death and mourning in the primary liturgical and theological space of the community.

We used this cycle often that winter. Karl, a priest diagnosed with AIDS, died in January. He had come to the church after his diagnosis and after his first major sickness: our parish became his family, his support, his daily providers, and his companionship. We had ministered to him daily for two years. His death was a serious blow to the community, not only because many people were involved over a long period with his care, but also because we had begun to believe that his chronic condition would last for many years and that, therefore, we would never need to face his death. Cumulatively these deaths were beginning to cause great pain in the community.

Then in February, George, the president of a theological school in the area, died suddenly and unexpectedly of a heart attack the day he returned from a sabbatical year. He was a middle-aged man who had written wonderful letters of anticipation at returning to the life and liturgy of the parish. His burial, following our now familiar custom, was a more public event. That was also the year that young Peter, a child whose life came to signify our own fragile lives, died from his leukemia. Young Peter was prayed over from his conception, through his gestation, at his birth, throughout his illness, and finally at his burial.

Four deeply troubling funerals took place in a short three-month period. By this time, the threat that grief would overwhelm the community was great. The rectors and parish leaders began to strategize about ways to address the grief. We feared that all our departed would become confused, conflated, and merged into a general depression and a sense of futility that would not allow us truly to grieve each one individually. We did not have time to grieve individually. Where would we begin?

I searched back into my own memory as a youth in the Greek Orthodox Church to the traditions that sustained our family in times of grieving. I recalled that time was set apart in the community to grieve: certain rituals and customs obtained for the first forty days of grieving, others at the anniversaries of three months, six months, a year, and every year thereafter. These Orthodox rituals focused on the gathered community to mourn with the immediate family of the mourners. In Greece, signs are put up throughout the village announcing the date and time of the memorial service so that everyone may gather, mourn, and support the family of the deceased.

In preparation for the forty-day memorial service, a special wheat product, called *kollyva* (the classical Greek word for boiled wheat), is produced by the community, brought to the church for the service, and then consumed by those who attended the memorial service. *Kollyva* is food that bears a multitude of symbolic structures. Those grieving boil wheat, then wash, rinse, and place it in white sheets and gently dry it by hand—the drying feels like gently drying a body; the sheets become a shroud. They then mix the dried wheat with bitter herbs (parsley and cumin) and sweet things (walnuts, sesame, raisins, pomegranate, and cinnamon). They then mound this mixture on a platter, and sift powdered sugar over it so that it evokes the image of a white, eternal body. The body is then decorated with words and symbols of life. Replicating the physical presence of the deceased, the mourners bring the *kollyva* into the church and place on a table in the sanctuary so that metaphorically and sacramentally they bring their beloved deceased back to the church again. After the liturgy of the day, the congregation gathers around this table and sings the memorial service in unison and chants prayers for the dead. The people pray, sing hymns, remember, often weep: they gather together the living and the dead. And then the assembly eats the rather pleasant-tasting *kollyva* at the reception in the deceased's honor.

The preparation of the *kollyva* takes about five hours. So during that time, the community of friends and family gather and talk about how quickly the time had passed, how unbelievable it is that the person has died, how painful the thought of familiar things has become, and all the other emotions and reactions that grieving people have. They also comfort one another, laugh, enjoy one another's company, and spend time simply living together in the knowledge of their mutual grieving. The *kollyva* provides a concrete reason for assembly, ensures a long period of time for preparation and conversation, and focuses the grieving upon a particular day and a particular service.

Our community learned to grieve, to talk about the various responses to death, to experience the anger and pain, to gather into one Body the pained body of some. This process gave grieving structure, meaning, direction, and parameters. It became a formative element in our community life. We learned how to live together in pain, how to cry together, how to work together for our common edification and upbuilding. We learned how to recognize our departed members as still remaining in our community, as still living in our social bodies. We learned much more than simply how to prepare a strange concoction and to do a new service; we were learning a spirituality of living and dying.

The rituals and ceremonies surrounding the burial and memorializing of the dead attended to the construction of a language for the social body of the parish. As individuals, our social bodies expanded to embrace the lives and deaths of those in the parish whom we knew and loved. In these rituals, the social body of the parish was given voice. That voice related to the often self-conscious and intentional association of particular people and their grieving with the ritual. It was not simply that we were adopting an Orthodox liturgy for the memorializing of the dead, but that we were finding ways of expressing our specific grief about Brian, Carl, George, and Peter. Each time we prepared the *kollyva* for others, they too were added to the corporate body and our words, our conversations, our connotations, expanded to include the specific discourse around the death of specific people. We were developing new liturgical expressions to supplement the limitations of our ecclesiastical forms and to embrace a new discourse that was happening around death and the memorial services for the departed. We were creating a new language within the parish.

Over time other parishes heard about our work and began to ask for our liturgies and services. We shared both our liturgies for the burial of the dead and the instructions on how to prepare *kollyva*. Each of those parishes developed their own language around the liturgies, which in all likelihood was very different from the language developed in my parish. That is precisely the point: each community must learn to develop its own language arising out of its own experience. Having stressed the probable differences among the various parishes using the same liturgies, I note the liturgies united us into a common discourse revolving about a common set of practices. Although the specific connotations of the words probably differed among the groups, the common denotative level of the liturgy and the memorial service united the parishes in a common practice.

This corporate formation in mourning points to three other central elements of corporate spiritual formation that deserve mention. First, this new memorial service and its preparation provided an opportunity for the community to gather to prepare for the liturgy and to celebrate a liturgy. Unless people are prepared through some process of investment in the liturgy, the liturgy itself usually cannot provide sufficient solidarity for the community to become cohesive. Providing an opportunity for the creation of this solidarity and investment prior to the liturgy and then actually manifesting that solidarity in liturgy is the basis for corporate spiritual formation. The formation of a common and rich language depends upon the intentional preparation for liturgy.

The second element necessary for corporate spiritual formation is a commitment to discourse. It is not simply the solidarity created but also the conversation about the realities of God and the realities of living that infuses the liturgy with its power and transformative effect. The conversation, however, must have sufficient substance and depth to include the innermost fears and pains that we as humans experience, and to include at the same time the personal and corporate exploration of the reality and presence of God, whose involvement might be known only in the most difficult experiences or whose involvement might be evident in splendor and mighty acts. The corporate body's commitment to discussing these divine and human matters, then, provides the substance and occasion for corporate spiritual direction by becoming the primary occasion for the corporate body to search out its own life and the life of God in its midst. It is the locus of corporate direction. The language that emerges from this discursive formation infuses vitality into the liturgical life of the parish, and it adds depth to the parish's narrative. The story that we tell about our life as a local Body of Christ compels a deep and richly connotative language and a deep and expansive narrative line to become the fabric of a parish's life.

The third element needed for corporate spiritual formation relates to the question of power: the corporate body must grant power to something outside itself that will be given authority within it. In the example of our memorial service, this power was granted to a liturgy from a different branch of Christianity—from my own social body—and to a process foreign to American culture. Its obligatory dimension in our parish context granted it power so that the corporate body, of necessity, had to come to terms with it and could not dismiss it. In most churches, the community grants power and authority to an agent outside the community in the form of Scripture or ecclesiastical obedience. In the case of the liturgies I have just described, power was given over to participants to create the deep language of their own discourse. The power to articulate and specify the connotative level of the common language was a shared power among those in the community. It began with an ecclesiastical authorization from the ministers of the parish, but then it quickly became a powerful tool in the lives of the members of the parish. For our parish, however, some of that power derived from the parish's narrative. We were empowered to do something different precisely because we had a history, a narrative, a story that told us of the diverse activities of people before us in the parish. Our narrative had been given power to lead us into new and different ways of living. That same narrative power enabled us also to redefine *family* and to move in myriad new ways essential to the vitality of our common life, even though our theological heritage was both traditional (as Anglo-Catholics) and socially radical (as part of the Oxford movement). Corporate spiritual formation develops a language and a medium through these elements of solidarity, commitment to discourse, and obligation.

Preparation for Liturgy: The Study of the Proper Lessons

I emphasized above that liturgy demands preparation. Participants need to be initiated into the common codes that the liturgy employs to transform the complex lives of the attendant people. Communication demands this. They also need to be initiated into the common culture of a community's liturgy. The preparation for liturgy may take a variety of modes. I would like to explore only one here.

For many years, in every parish in which I have been involved, I have, with interested members of the parish, prepared for liturgy by reading the Scripture lessons for the liturgy before they are read at the Sunday service. These groups (generally one early in the week in the evening and one later in the week in the morning) simply gather, read the lessons for a given Sunday (called the propers: that is, the appointed Scripture lessons for that Sunday), and discuss them both in relation to the historical context of the apportioned Scripture and in relation to the life of the parish community. The group then prays and celebrates the Eucharist. The conversation in the propers groups may move anywhere the Spirit or the members wish, and there are no expectations about staying to the immediate task. Often an off-focus comment spurs an interesting insight or observation.

Let me describe the process more thoroughly. The goal of the group's work is to celebrate a Eucharist that emerges from the community's discourse, that has sought out the Name of God peculiar to that week's lessons for the community (this is the liturgical Proper Preface), and that gathers the community's conversation about God's word to them into the stream of the history of salvation. Although this eucharistic prayer must be constructed by the priest in the Episcopal tradition, the prayer's construction must reflect the community's discourse either by directly addressing their conversation, or, as more frequently happens, by indirectly translating that conversation into the language of prayer and into the words that will recall their scriptural conversation in a new dimension.

When the group gathers, the lessons for the week are read serially. After each lesson, the group has an opportunity to discuss its history and its message (perhaps) to the original community, to explore provisionally parallels to their own times and parish, and to allow the lesson to mingle with the concerns and interests of the corporate body. Generally, with each lesson (if it is appropriate), the group will inquire about the call within the Scriptures to prayer and intercession, searching for the particular perspective on the world and on their prayer that the lessons may suggest. Similarly, the group will attend to the call to conversion and repentance suggested in the Scriptures, locating the pressure points for their own personal and corporate sin and seeking ways to repent of their sin. And the group will normally seek the direction of the lessons in exploring the call to the reconciliation of their personal, corporate, and cultural brokenness in order to bring to peace and reconciliation all within and outside the community that is at enmity. These four perspectives on the lessons (mirroring the service's Liturgy of the Word, Intercessions, Confession, and Peace) provide ample time and occasion for the exploration of the Scripture, for conversation about personal and corporate issues, and for interaction between the Scriptures and contemporary life.

The discussion forms one the first aspects of the conversation, the discussion of Scriptures; but this conversation is transformed into another genre: prayer. The corporate discourse should not end in analysis or understanding alone but in prayer, so the propers group turns its own conversation into prayer in the members' own intercessions, concerns, prophecies, confessions, and rededications. And these prayers, together with the discursive work of the corporate body, are offered to God in the bread and the wine of the Eucharist.

The priest then forms the Great Thanksgiving. A discussion of the genre of the Great Thanksgiving will help explain this crucial moment when the discourse, transformed into prayer and offered to God, becomes part of the history of God's salvation of the world. The Great Thanksgiving links the history of salvation from the creation of the world, through the covenant with Israel and the sacred words of the prophets, to the ministry, passion, and death of Jesus, and the work of the Holy Spirit in the church. Although the history of salvation has definite contours (creation, redemption, the work of Jesus, the Spirit in the church), the specific content of the prayer itself changes according to the emphasis and orientation of the community. The variety of these prayers in our Prayer Book attests to this. The fixed contours of the Great Thanksgiving, however, give the impression that this history of salvation remains a historical and a closed phenomenon, even though the section on the work of the Spirit in the church may come down to our own times (in the form of specific prayers for church leaders, prayers about the needs of the congregation, or remembrance of the dead). The work of the Spirit, however, connects the discourse of the corporate body to the tradition and history of the church, and it is in this section that the priest begins to translate the discourse about the lessons, and the prayers of the people and their offerings, into the continual activity of God in world history. The history of salvation as recited in the narrative of salvation history, then, did not end years ago but continues to our own day, and to the life of the local community as is rehearsed in the parish's own narrative. At this point, the community's narrative begins to develop its focus, not in isolation from the history of the church, but as a vital part of the history of the work of the Spirit in the world.

The formation of the corporate body's language, then, emerges from these three perspectives on the Word: the Word studied and mingled with life, the discourse about the Word transformed into prayer, and the prayer translated into the Great Thanksgiving and the history of salvation. The language develops discursively, prayerfully, and historically as expressive of the life of the corporate body in its particularity and in its connection to the larger church. With each week of preparation, one's ability to search the Scriptures and to understand them in their own historical setting and in the life of the local community increases so that facility with the use of Scripture becomes a normal part of Christian living. Likewise the scrutiny of the world as viewed through the prism of the Scriptures, and the scrutiny of the self as refracted through the Scriptures, develops exponentially: the connection of self, world, and Word becomes a familiar connection. And finally, the history of salvation becomes not a recitation of the past, but a living experience of the presence of God perduring throughout the life of the church and continuing into the life of the local community in its corporate body.

The Sermon

Not every member of the community, however, will be able to attend such intensive groups. The sermon at the Sunday liturgy transfers the fruits of this study to the congregation assembled. In the process of transferring this work to the larger corporate body, the sermon assists the congregation in developing a cohesive language about their life in the Spirit and their connection to each other and to God. The work of the preacher revolves about praying through the various levels and contents of the several discussion groups to create a vital word from God for the community. The sermon does not consist merely of the tabulation of concepts emergent from the community's life, nor of a teaching about the historical situation of the lessons from the Scripture. These matters are best communicated through study groups. The sermon, however, is the priest's refraction of these discussions through the priest's knowledge of the community, pastoral relations with individuals, corporate pastoral situations, the life of the world, and the priest's personal prayer about all of these. The sermon, in other words, works these propers-groups' material, and all the other information about the community, to produce fresh and vital words for the community that will lead the community to the same process of involvement with the Word of God, the transformative prayer of discourse, and the connection with the history of salvation, which converts the individual bodies in the community. The various discussions, along with other experiences and needs of the community and the world, become embedded in the preacher's life and produce a parallel, connected, and transformative parish discourse. This preaching, then, assists the parish to continue developing a language and a theology about the things of God. Another way of expressing this is that the sermon democratizes the discursive language of various groups of the parish. By refracting the Word through the various bodies in the church to galvanize the Body of Christ as a living entity, the sermon becomes a purveyor of communal language.

We have explored in this chapter the complexities of developing the language of angels, the particular language of prayer in a community. I want to underscore that these processes are complex and demand serious attention for corporate spiritual formation to occur. Here I started from the concept of a parish narrative and moved through individual, social, and corporate formative practices to develop a common language of prayer. I could have started at any one of these places and worked through to the other elements, because each of these elements in its own way opens the congregation to understanding its own religious and spiritual culture. Culture depends to a great extent on a common language; the formation of a new culture depends to a significant degree on the articulate and intentional formation of a common language. The depth of that common language will depend upon the adjoining of connotative meanings emergent from the community's own life to the denotative meanings received from tradition.

I call this *a language of angels* because my sense of this language is that it fills the air with depth. When communication among the participants of a community has rich depth and specificity, the levels of communication and the complexity of reality finds expression. The air becomes full of profound meaning. That strong communication, however, does not relate only to the people in the congregation but also to their relationship with God. The language is a language of prayer because in the end the discourse is with God. We learn through speaking to one another to speak with God, a God capable of speaking to us through a multiplicity of instruments: signs, people, and occasions. Parish communication in this way enhances the prayer life of the community and has a significant impact on the vitality and transformative quality of liturgy. The religious culture that we create through the connotative process of our language development becomes a culture attuned to the reality of God so that our speech is indeed a language of angels spoken in a culture formed around our relationship to God.

4

Power and Solidarity in Liturgy and Preaching

THE CONTOURS OF MY presentation of corporate spiritual formation through the liturgy has become gradually more complex. We began with culture as a frame for understanding liturgy, then moved to a simple theory of communication and then to a problematizing of the various bodies affected by liturgy, and finally to a description of language formation. At each turn, the theorizing has become more demanding. In this chapter, we move to even more complex concepts of power and solidarity as they operate in a community and affect the corporate spiritual formation of a parish. The chapter will bring together very disparate materials under this rubric and begin to lay out specific practices for community diagnostics and spiritual formation.

Grammar, Style, and Accents in Denominational Spirituality

My discussion of language looked at language only from the level of the denotative and connotative functions within the corporate body. It is time now to look at the larger structures that situate our use of words or signs. In moving toward these larger systems that create meaning, I leave aside the method I have used before, that of beginning with a specific experience and moving toward analysis. This chapter begins to do more explicitly theoretical work.

In contexts other than this book, *spirituality* commonly is understood as referring to the religious exercises, religious experiences, and moral formation of the individual person and thus generally concerns the personal appropriation and experience of faith.[1] As I argued earlier, spirituality has a social dimension because religious people also relate to religious communities of faith, and because members of religious communities speak to one another about their common faith and the means of living that faith corporately. Spirituality may also, then, be understood as part of the communication system within a parish or other religious community, and thus it may be understood as an interior system of communication about the experience of faithful living within a cohesive religious community.

So far in my discussion I have focused on the very local perspective on a community by looking primarily at experiences of people within a local community. This local perspective is necessary for corporate spiritual formation, but it is not the only level at which language functions. To explore only the local dynamics would remain myopic, and so I turn now to larger systems. Those larger systems, however, operate within the purview of the local liturgy; the local liturgy remains the site in which other larger systems, ones that I will call semantic systems, impinge and affect the local spirituality.

Let me step back a little to discuss denominational spirituality within Christianity. This discussion of denominational spirituality will assist us to understand how larger systems work. At the global level, Christian spirituality could be divided into three primary groups: Orthodox, Catholic, and Protestant. These global groups articulate distinct spiritual traditions. Yet even as we look closely at one spiritual tradition, the Protestant, we realize that under the global uniformity there stands a teeming diversity. There is in fact a diversity of Protestant spiritual traditions that found their expression in both the magisterial (Lutheran, Zwinglian, and Calvinist) and the national (English and Swedish) reformations beginning in the sixteenth century. Each Protestant denomination (along with geographical and theological varieties of Roman Catholicism, and ethnic and linguistic varieties of Eastern Orthodoxy) developed historically in different ways in different contexts, and also developed spiritually in distinctive and articulated ways—not only in relationship to other groups within its own denomination, but also in relationship to other varieties of religious people around them. Each denomination has developed a spirituality that functions as

1. See Bouyer, *History of Christian Spirituality*, vii–xi.

an interior system of communication for articulating its understanding of faithful living for members. Each Christian denomination has developed a language of its own for communicating its own identity and values, and this language functions analogously to the systems we have looked at in the local parish.

I can provide a very specific personal example. I was raised in the Greek Orthodox Church here in the United States, and I received an excellent religious formation under the guidance of some very devout women in my family (my grandmother, great-aunt, and mother), and under the direction of two very fine priests. I loved (and still love) the traditions of the Church that regulated the life of observant Orthodox Christians, and I was attentive to learn as much as I possibly could. Through a variety of circumstances, I left the Greek Orthodox Church after college. The reasons are not important, but the leaving was a matter of wanting to be part of a church that took my American identity as seriously as my Greek and Orthodox identity. I wanted, in short, to be a part of an independent American (and English-speaking) Orthodox Church. After leaving, I searched for a church that could allow me to retain my Orthodox training and yet would challenge me to be thoroughly American in my identity. Two serious options obtained: the Roman Catholic Church and the Episcopal Church. I chose, in the end, to become an Episcopalian.

Joining another denomination is not a matter of finding similar structures and beliefs and emphasizing them. Such similarities are important, of course, as a bridge, but they are also often deceptive. The test really revolves around differences: divergent ways of thinking, of organizing, of expressing, of metaphorizing the religious life and teaching. A transfer to a new denomination demands that the person accommodate these differences by identifying them and by assimilating them into a new way of living and experiencing God. It is very much like learning a new language as well as a new culture. These are the systems of communication that I am talking about: the systems that make, for example, an Episcopalian an Episcopalian (and not a Lutheran or a Presbyterian), and a Presbyterian a Presbyterian (and not a Methodist or Roman Catholic).

Now let me step even further back in order to introduce more explicitly theoretical language for our use. Semiotics is the study of signs. Semiotics looks at the signs: words, gestures, symbols that people use to communicate with one another. In a liturgy, for example, people using semiotic theory would analyze the entrance rite (as a procession from the rear of the church or simply a minister entering through a door into the sanctuary), the lessons that are read, the symbols (cross, candles, pulpit) that adorn the room, and any other sign that can be used to make meaning. Actually it might be better to say that semiotics studies the way that a sign differs from every other sign, and how that difference communicates meaning.[2] This means that the cross on the communion table does not mean the same thing as the offering plate. Their difference in function creates a difference in meaning. Social semiotics studies the production of signs in cultures, and explores the social environment in which meaning is produced, particularly around issues of social solidarity and the exercise of power.[3] Both semiotics and social semiotics use (at least distantly) linguistic models for understanding human communication. In the study of denominational spirituality, we might say that each denomination has developed a different sign system that communicates its spirituality. Although each sign system is different, generally common elements (such as Scripture, prayer, sacraments, styles of preaching, values, public worship, or rites of passage, for example) make up each system. These common elements of spirituality are combined, nuanced, put into context, and manipulated in such a way as to produce a specific meaning.

Using the linguistic metaphor for communication, grammar, style, and accent at once demarcates groups and enables them to communicate. Grammar distinguishes at the broadest level of linguistic organization: in the context of our global spiritual traditions, grammatical development would distinguish in historical sequence Eastern Orthodox, Roman Catholic, Lutheran, and other Reformation traditions, as well as the ethnic and racial groups that compose the largest systematic organization of spiritual material. Style functions as a subcategory of grammar to demarcate groups within a grammatical organization. There can, for example, be a great similarity between Romanian and Syrian Orthodox spirituality at the level of grammar, while simultaneously they might exhibit stylistic differences based on national, cultural, geographical, or other distinctions at the level of style. In communication a style is just such a combination of elements that, when put together, clearly demarcate one group from another. We can thus potentially articulate a style of spirituality indicative of Lutheran Christians, as we can articulate an Anglican style that would include Anglicans in England, Zimbabwe, Australia, and Canada, as well as

2. See Hodge and Kress, *Social Semiotics*; and Eco, *A Theory of Semiotics*, for discussions of semiotic theory.

3. Hodge and Kress, *Social Semiotics*, 82–91.

Episcopalians in the United States and Scotland. These styles of spirituality function as a cohesive agent: they create solidarity among a group of people around a commonly understood and articulated religious ideology, so that Lutherans from around the world will experience their common spiritual life, as will Anglicans, Orthodox, Catholics, Calvinists, and Anabaptists. There are differences within each of the stylistic groups, differences called accents, which distinguish alternative solidarities with the larger group. So high-church or Catholic accents may be known in Anglican, Lutheran, and Methodist styles of spirituality and be experienced within each separate group as a less central point of solidarity. Some of these accents may cross stylistic and grammatical lines and thus may appear in a variety of different environments where common practices create alternative expressions within various grammars and styles.

A denomination's spirituality presents systems whereby the solidarity of its members is created, and a commonly acceptable exercise of authority is maintained. Communication about spirituality actually is communication about the underlying systems of solidarity (between participants in a particular community and between members of a community and God). Communication about spirituality is also communication about the exercise of power (who has divine power and how such power is modulated among the various members of the community). The style of spirituality describes the interior relationship of its people. Style describes the solidarity in relationship to itself. People within a particular style may recognize one another and know the meaning of the spiritual signs. Style clearly differentiates one group from another. A member of a stylistic group immediately recognizes those people who do not speak the same language, and knows immediately that the foreign speaker is not one of us. Style creates a system of solidarity.

Much in the early part of this book relates to the development of solidarity. My interest has focused, in other words, on the question of developing and maintaining a style of liturgy that marks the style of a local parish's communication. The importance of creating a culture, of articulating the complexities of the bodies, and of creating a language relates primarily to the question of solidarity. I have introduced these subjects in order to provide the substance of a system of solidarity that unites the disparate members of a religious community. Correlative to questions of solidarity, as semiotics and social semiotics maintain, stand also questions of power. A group of people who have formed a solid union manifest a system of power that defines simultaneously both their association and their relationship to people outside the association. Solidarity and power stand together as aspects of corporate spiritual formation through the liturgy.

In the remainder of this chapter, I will explore the dual questions of solidarity and power as they are manifest in the liturgy and in the work of the leaders and participants in worship. These perspectives will significantly advance our understanding of the complexity of corporate spiritual formation.

The Liturgical Context as a Diagnostic Tool

Using solidarity and power as lenses through which to explore liturgy, let me describe a typical Sunday Liturgy of the Word at my first parish. This constitutes a kind of diagnostic reading that I hope will model similar diagnostic readings in other religious community environments.

The Gathering of the Corporate Body

Liturgy begins as various people assemble. Long before anyone sits in a pew, a number of people have already begun to work: the organist to practice music and to play a prelude to the service; the choir director and choir to rehearse their contribution; the acolytes and servers, who vest and make sure all the furniture and props are in place; the members of the altar guild, who light the candles and prepare various elements of the service; the lay leaders of the liturgy, who have vested and have come prepared to read or to pray in the service; and the ordained ministers, who have vested and come prepared to lead the service. Most of these people have assigned and separate seats in the front of the liturgical assembly, often on a platform higher than those seated in pews, and they often face outward to the larger assembly.

At the back of the church, greeters assist the congregation in finding seats in pews and distribute a printed bulletin, a sheet of information that assists the general participants to follow the service. The general congregant takes a seat facing forward toward the sanctuary where the leaders of the liturgy will sit. They listen to music, while also reading the announcements in the bulletin and generally open their hymnal to the first hymn that they will sing.

Where a person sits in a worship service defines both solidarity and power. There is a sociality related to leading public worship as an acolyte, a lay reader, a choir member, or a vested minister. Clothing distinct from normal street clothes, or assigned seating at the head of the assembly, defines their solidarity and visually sets them apart as guiding agents of the liturgy. Their solidarity expresses their power: these participants will be able to speak, read, walk around, and sing as authorized leaders of the liturgy. They bear all the markings of power. The majority of people, however, sit together in the pews, seldom speak apart from other members of the congregation, have undesignated seating, and wear normal street clothes. They have solidarity with each other, but their power remains a shadow of the vested people who sit in the sanctuary. This unequal power situation receives ritual enactment when the vested ministers, after all the congregants are seated, process into the church singly or in pairs to take their authoritative seats.

The gathering of the community plays out the significance of location and seating in the church, while simultaneously marking out the power dynamics. At the apex of this locational system stands the leader of the liturgy, set out both by marks of ecclesiastical and academic authority. The gathering, then, follows somewhat predictable patterns of hierarchy and power in the relations of various participants.

Opening or Processional Hymn

The liturgy rehearses the unity of the entire liturgical assembly by beginning with a hymn that is sung by all. This unitary voice disrupts and displaces the hierarchy established by seating and attempts to create a common focus through common singing. The hymn indicates a solidarity and univocality within the assembly that at once are independent of and mask the various demarcations of power indicated by the seating arrangement. Although there are distinctions of power and authority, music creates the image that such distinctions are not essential to the gathering. Music both creates solidarity and interjects an alternative power into the liturgical performance.

The Beginning of the Liturgy

Everything that has preceded this point has been preparatory. Although semiotically the liturgy began much earlier than at this point, textually and officially the opening prayers, recitations, and invocations of God constitute the beginning of the liturgy. These invocations begin with the work of the liturgical president, the (usually ordained) person who presides over the liturgy and serves as the chief authority for its function.

The shift from music to speech dramatizes the focus of power. Music created the image of shared power and authority in marked contrast to the opposite message of the seating arrangements. From the area of restricted and designated seating, one voice among many begins the liturgy by invoking God. In the question of voice, the single voice bears the greatest power, while multiple voices (as in responsorial statements and singing) bear the least liturgical power. And among the single voices, those voices that have the capacity to speak spontaneously are more powerful than those single voices that may only speak prescribed texts. The expressions at the very beginning of the liturgy lay out the entire system of modulated power in the liturgical assembly.

The Reading of Lessons

Someone (either clergy or lay) closer to the source of power and authority (the front of the church) rises to read a sacred text; that is, a text that has been designated as revelatory for the community and authorized by someone for public reading. The relative power of the reader rests on being able to speak as one voice only, but that power is modulated by the designation of the text that the single-voiced person may read. It could be Scripture, poetry, or any other kind of reading that the community, at whatever level (the parish, the denomination, or some subset of both), has deemed significant to reveal God to the assembly.

The authority of the text is aligned semiotically with the authority of the liturgical leaders and the greater proximity to God by being situated at the front of the assembly in the sanctuary. One of the ways that denominational power finds expression in the local liturgy revolves about the authorized lessons, for those churches that use a common lectionary; and one way the minister expresses his or her solidarity with the denomination is by the use of such denominationally authorized texts for public reading in local assemblies under the minister's care. Conversely, in those denominations that do not use a common lectionary, great power is given to the leader who is the single voice who chooses the reading for the day.

The voice of the reading speaks with authority and power, as does the content of the reading. Everyone, including the vested participants in the sanctuary, listen attentively, receiving the authorized sacred text as passive members listening actively (or so it is hoped). The central focus of reading these texts displays its power within the community and also creates again a solidarity among all those who listen attentively to texts to which all must submit.

The Sermon

The sermon pushes the dynamics of solidarity and power to their furthest extreme. The preacher, set apart from all others, speaks univocally. All others, including those empowered to sit in the sanctuary and to be vested participants, remain silent and give full attention to the speaker. The preacher stands out from the solidarity created with the liturgical assembly and thereby breaks the sense of uniformity and community to speak from without. The speaker's power derives from this break in solidarity. The voice of the preacher receives status and priority to speak on behalf of the community, to the community, and representing a kind of divine voice resonating through the community's life. Despite the discomfort that many preachers feel around this aura of divine authority, the aura nonetheless exists and is played out semiotically Sunday after Sunday. The preacher's words reflect, communicate, and transfer divine presence into the corporate body of the assembly. Congregations even expect laypeople, when they preach, to portray this sense of sermon as numinous encounter. The preacher thus functions both as the minister's voice and that of God's.

This investment of divine power with a consequent break in community solidarity occurs also in churches that do not have a strong tradition of preaching, such as in the Roman Catholic and the Eastern Orthodox churches. What the priest says represents not simply the mind of the priest, but the acceptance of the will and understanding of God or of God's church. The words carry a meaning and importance far beyond the words of simply one person. The assumption of divine presence pervades the process even outside the Protestant tradition with its strong emphasis on the liturgy and preaching of the Word.

Most Protestant congregations understand the sermon as the high point or apex of the liturgy. Anything that follows the sermon functions as denouement, the release of the dramatic tension of revelation achieved in the sermon. In more Catholic circles, the sermon serves as the apex of the first part of the liturgy, the Liturgy of the Word, and prepares the way for the Liturgy of the Sacrament. The Sermon thus represents the first peak in a dually valued process of Word and Sacrament. However, in both Protestant and Catholic circles, the sermon represents the voice of God delivered specifically to the assembly gathered. Communities expect God's voice to be different, particular, unique to the gathering. The sermon achieves this particularity of God's word to the community by interpreting the sacred text for the community and by applying its significance to the life of the social and corporate bodies of the assembly.

The goal of the sermon within the frame of the liturgy is to call the assembly to conversion of life, to present an understanding of the way of life to which they are called, to open roads of transformation and renewal of life within their given life situation, and to open their minds to see and to understand the voice of God in their own context. The preacher may only achieve this by first creating a deep sense of solidarity with the community through active participation in the liturgy that precedes the sermon, and then liturgically or ritually breaking that solidarity by stepping forward as the sole voice interpreting the text to the community. The power of the preacher's voice comes from a system of solidarity created through the minister's ordination, which links the minister to church authority and to divine authority. The preacher's power thus stands at odds with the solidarity created in other parts of the liturgy and in other aspects of ministry. The preacher's power is anomalous to the preacher's life situation by virtue of the necessity to break the established solidarity for the purpose of preaching the Word. I will deal with this more fully later, but let me finish with the diagnostic reading of the Liturgy of the Word.

Prayers, Confession, Peace, and Announcements

The assembly has been silent through the sermon. In response to the sermon and to their own hearing of the Word, and as a means of re-creating the solidarity with the preacher that had been broken during the preaching of the sermon, the community begins its intercessory prayer. Intercession may include also the confession of corporate and individual sin and end with the exchange of peace. The process reflects the need to establish a strong sense of the solidarity of the corporate body. The minister, together with the people, turn their attention to communication with God through prayer. Solidarity is reestablished and the community is restored to its full sense of functioning as the Body of Christ.

This diagnostic reading shows the complexity of the systems supporting the sermon's communication. My language of the social and corporate bodies may help to make the system of communication more accessible.

61

The sermon works on the individual in a corporate setting, or, more specifically, the sermon addresses the social body in the context of the corporate body. The sermon transfers the reality of the corporate body to the social body of the participant in the liturgy. In this way, the sermon translates material from the larger body to the smaller, from the corporate body of the corporate assembly to the social body of the person listening.

Reading and Interpreting Sacred Text

Before exploring more fully the role of the sermon and the preacher to the communicative process, let me take up a prior question that relates to the sacred text read at the liturgy.

In the context of liturgy, sacred text stands as a revelatory agent: The function of reading the text is to reveal the presence of God in the community. The text makes present and immediate the historical revelation of God, whether that history is something written just before the service or whether that history is the Bible written over the course of thousands of years. The text is from outside the local corporate body, and thus it is grafted onto the corporate body through the ears, through listening and interpreting, and through reacting to what is heard. Sacred readings, then, introduce the other, the outside, the foreign, into the corporate body as a historical element of the corporate body, a historical element that can only be remembered if it is reinforced through public reading. Even in communities of charismatic Christians or in other churches with a developed theology of the presence of the Holy Spirit within the participants—churches that locate God in their corporate body—the sacred texts transfer historical revelations to the revelation taking place in the community.

The authority of the text is conferred by the gathered assembly and is renewed at every gathering. It is not self-evident authority, or obvious, but rather an authority carefully rehearsed in the attitudes and reactions of the corporate body in liturgical assembly by various ritual acts that set it apart. In my first parish, two candles were carried on either side of the Bible (the book was ceremonially carried high above everyone's head in procession), then the book was incensed and the gospel was chanted by a single voice in the midst of the assembly of people. The signs were clear that this was an authoritative text each time it was read or chanted. All such liturgical actions reestablish the authority of sacred text to reveal God in whatever form to the local corporate body.

The authority to interpret the sacred text is also one conferred by various signs. The authorized interpreting body may be retained by the community as a whole (as in a monastic setting) or conferred upon a member of the local body (as in a congregational setting) or conferred by a larger external hierarchical structure (as in Roman Catholic, Anglican, Orthodox, and Lutheran circles, for example). Or there may be a magisterium of theologians and other religious professionals whose primary work is to provide the acceptable and ecclesially consistent interpretation for those to whom they confer the power of local interpretation.

Sacred texts raise the important question about when and where God is revealed: If revelation is understood to have happened many years ago, and to be a closed system to which modern people must submit, then the text stands in the community as the closed system of God's revelation. The text defines the presence. If, on the other hand, revelation is understood to take place in the context of the corporate assembly, then the text provides indicators to the modern community about the recorded history of God's revelation as an aid to the community's own revelation. The critical issues of ordination (who has authority to interpret) and initiation (when and where is God revealed in the community and by whom) converge in the process of interpreting sacred text. Another issue, the importance of the historical context to the creation and formulation of the sacred text, also becomes important, because the presumed context of the writing of sacred text bears different weight depending upon the manner in which the text is understood to reveal God.

All these aspects of reading and interpreting sacred text, whether in the sermon itself or simply in the liturgy, relate to the degree of God's revelation made possible in the corporate body of the assembly. The question of the degree of revelation relates also to the construction of the real and the true in the corporate body.

The Sermon as an Instrument of Complex Communication in the Corporate Body

The complex system of communication I have just described focuses on the sermon and its function of translating material from the corporate body to the social body. What is the material translated? This is actually very complex because it focuses so many different aspects on one function: the sermon. First, the sermon translates sacred text and the authorizing agency for the reading of sacred texts; the sermon not only makes the text that was read in the liturgy accessible to the congregation, but it also simultaneously activates the authority of the agency that stipulated which texts may be read in the assembly. This is subtle. Let me take the Bible as the example. The sermon takes a Bible passage and engages a community's life with it. This is the obvious level of translation: the preacher takes the text that has been read and makes it part of the lives of the assembled people. But some agent had to decide that the Bible should be authorized as a revelatory text, as opposed to some other text like the Constitution of the United States or the Quran. Whenever that authorized text is read in the liturgy, the authorizing agency exercises its power and authority in the assembly. Although hidden and implicit, the denomination or Church tradition or the Board of Deacons—whoever makes the decision that a particular text like the Bible will be the revelatory text for the liturgy—exercises authority over the assembly. But it is not simply the exercise of the authority regarding texts, but also the exercise of authority in stipulating who may interpret the text for the assembly through the ordination of authorized preachers for the community, or in the raising up lay preachers for some denominations with no external ordination process. The occasion of the sermon manifests a variety of power structures: the agency that authorizes revelatory texts, the agency that ordains particular people to interpret the text to a specific community, and the position of the preacher who has received a call from a congregation to serve as its interpretative minister. The first two authorizing agencies create solidarity between the preacher and those agencies, such as the denomination, or the ordaining body. The relationship of the preacher or minister to the community creates an unequal but close relationship of preacher to parish. The sermon exhibits divided loyalties for the preacher, who in turn relates to a denomination, a sacred text, a system of ordination, and a congregation of people all at once. The sermon, therefore, remains a very carefully negotiated space for the exercise of power and authority and for the creation of solidarity among the preacher's various explicit and implicit connections. This may provide one explanation of the reason that some people leave a parish when a new minister arrives: they have not yet established solidarity with the new minister (and are still relying upon their solidarity with the previous minister) and, therefore, they do not accept the new minister's authority and power in their lives or in the community.

The ambiguity of the preacher's position within the community also functions as a means of translating information and community identity from the corporate body to the social body of the individual. With the responsibility of making the revelatory text accessible to the social body, the sermon also translates corporate systems of interpretation from the world outside the community to those present within the community. The sermon provides a bridge between the outer worlds instantiated in the complex allegiances of the preacher and the world of the community. The sermon functions as a bridge because it presents the values that the corporate body upholds: values about the sacredness of the revelatory text, values about the role and function of the preacher, values about the larger systems of power and authority relative to the local community, values about the relationship of the sermon to the social body's politics and social location, values about all the other systems that create solidarity between the various elements of the corporate body, and values about the relationship of the parish to the wider external community in which it exists. The sermon communicates this with the authority of the corporate body and thereby it creates solidarity. To the extent that the assembled social bodies resonate positively with this authority, strong solidarity will be created; while to the extent that the assembled social bodies resonate negatively, weak solidarity will result. These questions of solidarity emergent from the sermon influence the status of membership and participation of each social body in the assembly. The sermon also translates diagnostic information to the corporate body by presenting the community with a mirror by which its life can be evaluated and assessed. The preacher may present this diagnostic information through direct content: through style, form, humor, and gestures. Observe, for example, what is considered humorous in a sermon and you will discover what communal attitudes and values that community holds.

So how does the sermon accomplish all this? The producer of the sermon reads and evaluates two obvious texts and one hidden one. The obvious texts are first the text of the sacred writings and second, the text written in the corporate body of the liturgical assembly. In the sermon the exegetical, theological, social, and political messages of the sacred text and the diagnostics of the life of the local community meet. And the hidden text is the life (both immediate and known through the community narrative) of the producer of the sermon. The preacher's life provides the hermeneutical context for the production of a sermon: personal issues, prejudices, political stances, hopes and fears, vestry problems, unresolved anger, joy—all these elements provide the lens through which both obvious texts travel in order to be communicated to the assembly. Ultimately the sermon becomes the corporate body, filtered through the social body of the preacher, and communicated to the social body of the listeners. And in becoming the corporate body, the sermon creates the solidarity necessary for forming a sense of intimate and vital community cohesion. This produces a complete circle from the community to the community, through the social body of the preacher.

Communication in the Corporate Body—
Preacher, Sermon, and Community

When we begin to put these complex systems of power and solidarity together, an even more complex discourse emerges. This communication focusing on the sermon remains very complex. Three major players participate in this system: the corporate body of the community constituting the majority of the assembly, the social bodies of the members of that corporate body constituting an even larger group than those present in the assembly, and the social body of the preacher within the corporate assembly.

I will begin with the description of the preacher's social body, because in many respects it is the lens that presents the greatest challenge. The social body of the preacher consists of a wide network of interrelated relationships that begin with her own family, friends, and acquaintances outside her connections to the parish. Her social body also includes civic leaders, denominational leaders, and peers in the professional ministry; these are all the professional relationships that a minister develops not only in the local community but also in the wider sphere of her professional life. The preacher's social life also embraces her life in the local parish where she has generally come as an outsider to live at the center of a community. Her role as minister in a parish extends her social body into the lives of the members of the parish; she brings all the diverse spiritual, intellectual, pastoral, administrative, liturgical, and other relationships that have developed with members of the parish through her day-to-day work. Intellectual curiosity and good education have molded her social body intellectually, and generally the minister has more years of higher education than most people in her parish. Although generally better educated, the minister usually receives a lower monetary compensation than most members of the parish. She comes to her community as a leader and as a servant: she leads the community as the designated leader, and yet depends upon the community for financial support, professional success, and spiritual growth.

She is intimately involved in the lives of the members of her parish because she knows their illnesses, their failures, their brokenness, their marital and sexual problems, their financial worries, their concerns over children, and all the minute aspects of her parishioners' lives that connect with their spiritual development. Although the minister stands capable of communicating the intimate detail of her own life and the lives of her parishioners, the community expects her not to reveal the intimacies that she knows and not to act on the basis of her knowledge of other people's lives. The community also expects that she will not act solely on the basis of her own perspective and prejudices. In this sense the community understands the minister to be value-free, neutral, and without prejudice, even though that expectation cannot be met by any member of the community. This brief description of the social body of the minister shows how complex the minister's social body remains, and that complexity becomes the lens that communicates the understanding of the community's life and its sacred texts.

The same level of complexity and interrelatedness, stripped of its specifically ministerial context, applies to the social bodies of every member of the parish. The community also represents a vast network of connections, reactions, neuroses, mental problems, educational levels, social statuses, professions, and professional networks. The corporate body is no simple body to construct, and communication within such a corporate body presents great challenge.

In an earlier chapter I discussed the concept that one function of the liturgy is to create a common language among its participants. That common language now may be understood in its richest form from the perspective of the various social bodies present in the liturgical assembly and from the perspective of the complex corporate body that the liturgical assembly solidifies. The common language emerges from the associations, meanings, referents, connotations, experiential referents, emotional connections, and other systems of meaning constructed through the words in order to communicate with their specific referents within this specific corporate body. The liturgy does not function as a kind of dictionary for the articulation of meaning, but rather the liturgy provides the arena in which the specific lives of specific people in a particular liturgical assembly construct and develop the meaning of words, gestures, music, smells, and physical locations (among many other elements). The communication in the corporate body uses language for its discourse. Although this language has a context outside the liturgy, the liturgy enables the words to develop specific meaning in the context of the corporate body. For example, a raised hand in the context of a worship service may signify a blessing, but in another context it could be a Nazi salute. Likewise, shaking hands in a business context means something different from shaking hands as part of a liturgical kiss of peace. The rich verbal and nonverbal, gestural, musical, and locational meanings derived from those living together in a community form a rich fabric of sustained corporate communal systems. These communicative systems form, develop, and undergird the life of the community; such systems function as a kind of blood system to the corporate body, carrying life and oxygen to the whole body.

The sermon creates the atmosphere in which all these aspects of language development happen. The sermon inaugurates the discourse that makes the corporate body live. The discourse within a specific community, now using the corporate body's own language system, enables that community to live gracefully and deliberately as part of one cohesive corporate body with a common language. The discourse established by the sermon gathers up all the individual social bodies and knits them into a corporate body, giving language to the various discourses occurring in the community. In this way the sermon gives a voice to the corporate body. The sermon gives speech and communication to the community.

As it embodies the voice of the corporate body, the preacher's voice carries great authority and responsibility. The questions of power and authority, which social-semiotic theory presents, come to the fore because these questions modulate the preacher's voice. With whom does the preacher identify? Where is the solidarity created with the community? Is solidarity expressed with the people, with the leadership of the parish, with the people not present in the liturgical assembly? And where does the power come from? How is power modulated? All the factors locate the preacher's social body in relationship to the other social bodies in the assembly and to the corporate body as a whole. The preacher's perspectives and attitudes, whether intentionally or not, will determine the health of the life of the corporate body. It is a sole and powerful voice that may give life or death to the corporate body, depending upon the preacher's ability to process the life of the community.

The sermon remains both complex and vital in its communication within the corporate body, and the preparation of the sermon takes on a similar complexity. The sermon is no simple process of interpretation of a sacred text; such a simplistic view disregards the questions about the modulation of power and the relationships of solidarity that we have been exploring. In circumstances where the sermon is understood primarily as the preacher's personal work, the preparation treats the congregation primarily as empty vessels to be filled by the superior knowledge of the preacher. This remains hierarchical and indicates a low level of solidarity with the hearers of the sermon. In circumstances where the sermon reflects simply the assembled people's opinions returned to them through the sermon, the sermon creates high solidarity within the corporate body but causes a diminishment of corporate spiritual growth and interactive communication. Such sermons take the excitement out of hearing and responding to God's renewing presence.

Neither of these two extremes works for producing a sermon. The sermon must arise in the discourse generated within the corporate body. The sermon must become a disciplined, deliberate, and articulate communication process involving the three primary bodies: the social body of the preacher, the social bodies of individual parish members, and the corporate body of the liturgical assembly. This communication cannot be produced in isolation from the interpretative community; it is not a theoretical set of relationships but a practical one. The community and its interpretation of sacred text must have a voice, a presence, and an ability to structure the contours of the sermon.

5

Gangs, Monks, and Workouts

Asceticism in Theory and Practice

IN THE PREVIOUS CHAPTERS we have explored a number of diagnostic tools for understanding community life. We have explored the formation of a culture, the development of language and community narrative, and the interrelationship of solidarity and power in community. Much of what I have analyzed has been particular experiences in parish life that have been the fodder for critical evaluation and reflection. In this chapter, I move toward a more proactive community formation situated in a theory of asceticism, which I will define and explore with you. I will begin with this theory of asceticism to examine how we may conceptualize the spiritual formation of individuals and communities by theorizing the process of formation itself.

But before we get to proactive asceticism as a means of formation, we need to think about systems of formation in general. We are continually being formed, from our youth onward, in social systems that regulate our lives. We are formed to be students in an educational system, formed to be children in a family system, formed to stand in line in order at the bus stop, formed in the proper way of eating a meal, formed to be political agents in society, formed in what it means to be a man or a woman, formed to know what a family should be, formed in proper means of mourning the dead and expressing grief, formed in acceptable expressions of emotions, formed in whom we consider blood relatives, and formed to be a professional worker or to be a blue-collar employee. We are implicated in a wide assortment of systems of formation to which we do not generally pay attention. But the formation is happening even though we may not be aware of it, and we are being formed to be particular kinds of people by the society in which we live. I would call these systems of formation *unintentional formation*, because they operate in the normal process of being socialized in any community or society.

Asceticism, however, raises the question of *intentional formation*. Intentional formation is that formation taken on by an individual or a community in order deliberately to create a certain kind of person or a particular kind of community. For example, orientation at a college is a system of intentional formation intended to lay out the guidelines for a successful college experience in a particular college. Every college's values and intentions are different, so the orientation lays out a systematic overview of the successful college graduate from that institution. The college orientation teaches incoming students about the atmosphere and values of the college community.

Another example of intentional formation is the process of learning how properly to drive an automobile. After learning the mechanics of gears, acceleration, and stopping, the driver must be formed in the systems and conventions of driving. These conventions are essential for a successful driver: stop at a red light and stop sign, signal the intention to turn left or right, stop behind school buses, keep a safe distance from other automobiles, observe weather conditions and make accommodations in the manner of driving, pay attention to other drivers, and do not text while driving. There are many more. The proper and successful driver will be formed in these systems so that she may function successfully as a driver.

Religious institutions engage in intentional formation, although I suspect that most religious institutions have not thought about formation very much. To be a religious person means critically to appraise the systems of unintentional formation and socialization and intentionally to chart a new direction in living and relating that contrasts with the received systems. To be a religious community demands the same critical appraisal of received and unintentional formation in order to chart an intentionally new direction for the community and its members. When religious institutions take intentional formation seriously, they enter the arena of asceticism.

Asceticism and Formation

I belong to a gym. I am not unlike many people in contemporary America—probably millions of people—who pay out their monthly and yearly membership fees to get themselves into shape. It is not a pleasant experience but a necessary one. Working out is almost a religion. In fact, I suspect that more people work out than go to church. Certainly many go to the gym two or three times a week and to church only once a week. Anyway, working out is a phenomenon that is part of our society that we need to explore for its intentionally formative impact.

I live in a city, an urban center. The neighborhood I live in reflects the life of a city in renewal: it is racially integrated, economically diverse (from the very poorest to the most wealthy), ethnically inclusive, religiously expansive, and includes people from a wide variety of lifestyles (elders, gay and lesbian couples, traditional families with children, singles, young married couples). We are a neighborhood trying to become a new kind of community, rich in diversity and strong in common identity. Our neighborhood intentionally forms us to be a particular kind of community by virtue of the choice to live there.

As I look around the city, however, the most successful people at creating community and sustaining membership in communities are the gangs that our neighborhood fears so much. Gangs have figured out how to embrace someone who is malleable or formable, who does not have a system of support or strength, who lacks self-confidence and trust in others, who needs other people to find completion, who lacks financial resources, and who seems generally lost. Gangs know how to embrace these people, how to include them in their community and provide them with not only a personal and group identity but also the financial and social support necessary for them to live well. Gangs have figured out an intricate system of intentional social and psychological formation, and they have applied it successfully not only in local settings but also now in national groupings.

Gyms and gangs point toward the realization in modern times of a truth that the church, especially the ancient church, has always known: people must be trained to be the people they aspire to be. In ancient Christianity, new Christians were not just converted once and let go. They were carefully molded and developed as new people, with new identities in radically new social relationships, and with a significantly different understanding of and relationship to God. They learned how to live as Christians over years of formation before they were even baptized: their minds, bodies, and lives were transformed over many years until they were capable not only of understanding the Christian life but living it. When they were properly formed (or reformed, perhaps), then they were ready for baptism. The early church trained Christians in mind, body, and life. And then, as when the persecutions of the late third and early fourth centuries, when hard times hit, Christians had the resources to maintain their individual and corporate identity with grace and integrity.

Our modern gangs have figured this out especially well. They do not accept people. They train people. They, like the monks of old, give people a particular costume or tattoo that marks their new identity; they demarcate themselves from other identifiable groups in the culture and use that demarcation as a means of sustaining and developing their strong internal ties; they provide for one another's social, financial, and spiritual needs; and they form a strong and cohesive, identifiable community of support. I could continue the comparison, but I think you understand my point. Intentional formation (whether of the body in the gym, of the participant in a neighborhood, or of a member of a gang) is a critical factor in our society, and in the traditional language of theology *formation* means asceticism. These examples portray similar processes of formation: they work with people to become a new person, they provide their participants with encouragement and direction, they promulgate concrete behaviors intended to be lifelong and satisfying, and they successfully produce the sorts of people that they set out to produce.

The ancient context of asceticism was sport: asceticism was physical training for combat in sport. In the same way that a fine athlete trains to become a winning competitor, so have ascetical processes formed people to become successful types of people. I am interested in looking at how this training happens in any dimension of living, whether religious or secular.

A Definition of *Asceticism*

Let me now step back and begin to put a theoretical and definitional frame to my topic, asceticism. In an article first published in the *Journal of the American Academy of Religion,* I developed the following definition of asceticism: "performances within a dominant social environment intended to inaugurate a new subjectivity, different social relations, and an alternative symbolic universe."[1] The theory revolves around five primary elements: an alternative perspective to a dominant environment, intentional performances, the articulation of a new subjectivity, the reorganization of social

---

1. Valantasis, "Constructions of Power in Asceticism." See also Valantasis, "A Theory of Asceticism, Revised."

relationships, and the reorientation of the symbolic universe. Let me take each one up in sequence.

An Alternative Perspective to a Dominant Environment

In classical language and metaphor, ascetics withdrew from the dominant culture in order to live an alternative lifestyle. Some ascetics withdrew from the inhabited world to the desert, others from the village to the forest, others from the public life of the urban center to a contemplative life apart from others in the city. Although it has traditionally been understood negatively, withdrawal simply creates a space within a dominant social and intellectual environment for working on something new. Withdrawal creates the opportunity for intentional training for something different. I withdraw from my normal world to enter the gym, a constructed world where I can develop the "new me." Gangs withdraw from their dominant culture to create an alternative and subversive one. What is important is the creation of an alternative space in which a new person may be formed and where new spiritual practices may be performed.

Intentional Performances

In the arts, performance theory articulates the methods and means of developing a "character." Richard Schechner, a performance theorist, describes a process of breaking down experiences into the smallest "malleable bits" of human expression in order to put them back together as a character.[2] The character's reality depends upon the actor creating minute details of speech and action that signify the character's personality and manner of living. This is an intentional process of training to become someone different, someone else, because it does not help to understand or even to conceptualize a character if that character cannot become real on the stage. The details, the malleable bits are what make the character real and believable. The better the actor is in performing these malleable bits of character, the more convincing the character becomes to the audience.

In antiquity, monks practiced their performances: they fasted intensively, battled with demons, resisted their thoughts and temptations, and abused their bodies to make them submit to higher reason. In modern

2. Schechner, *Performance Theory*, 6.

74

times, gang members learn specific and identifiable behaviors and signs that mark them out as different from all others. Members of a gang recognize themselves as being part of an intentionally constructed society. At the gym, I learn repeatable sequences that make me a new person through continued repetition, all to music that normally I abhor. These are the malleable bits of human expression that create or re-create the person.

One more aspect of intentional performance needs comment. Performances are public; they take place in front of other people. In the case of some of our desert monks that public stance, that performance, could be understood as taking place before a watchful God, or even as the emergent personality performing before a rejected personality. Even though members of the gym say they are not watching each other, they are, as do the trainers and owners of the gym. And gangs certainly scrutinize themselves and other gangs very carefully. The public nature of intentional performance creates the social space in which the new person may emerge and in which the new person may function.

The Articulation of a New Subjectivity

A subject is a person authorized to function in a society. For clarity's sake, I will simply use the term *identity*. Asceticism builds a new identity. A person who becomes dissatisfied with the options presented in the dominant culture withdraws from it in order intentionally to become or create a new identity. Gang members want to become other kinds of people, with strong corporate identities and social markers, with intense support both emotional and financial. The monk, no longer just a regular Christian, wants to become a monk, live like the angels, enter a new commonwealth. Asceticism enables the given identities to be discarded in favor of some alternative.

The issue of a new identity is an important one. We are given identities from very early in our lives by both family and society, and we tend to live those identities, those subjectivities, without reflection, and generally without combating them until something in our lives forces us to review and examine our way of being and of living. These given subjectivities are often limited by our social standing, education, families, and by the communities in which we live. In order to create a new identity, to become a different sort of authorized person in society, we must intentionally envision the new person that will replace the old. And when the new person is envisioned, we then develop the performances that will allow the new person to emerge and to thrive.

—*unchanged* ?

The Reorganization of Social Relationships

A new identity calls forth new social relationships. One cannot become a new person while maintaining the complex social web that defined the old way. Relationships among members of a gang must necessarily be different from relationships with other people; members of a religious society act differently with one another than they do with nonmembers or non-religious people. The social reorganization recognizes that a social nexus accompanies every articulation of identity, so that the desire to construct a new identity demands a consequent change in social relationships.

Alcoholics Anonymous and their affiliate organizations understand this aspect of asceticism well. Their meetings, scheduled throughout the day and week, offer an opportunity for socialization and deep conversation with other similar people who are working at creating a new, sober self. Their meetings provide the social support necessary to inaugurate and support this new identity as a sober person. And the discussions at the meeting assist the recovering alcoholic in reorganizing and reestablishing their communities of support, including their families. Without such social support, the new identity as a sober person would be difficult, if not impossible.

A new subjectivity demands reorganized and supportive social support. The new identity needs to relate to other people in different ways—ways appropriate to the new identity emerging from ascetical activity. Without such support, the new identity falters, often reverting to the social patterns of the old, rejected identity.

The Reorientation of the Symbolic Universe

The symbolic universe provides the structural justification for an identity and a set of social relationships. The symbolic universe develops the systems that explain the *why* and the *how* of a way of living. If one develops a new identity and enters into different social relationships that support that new identity, then one must articulate the rationale of that new identity, the worldview that enables that identity to be articulated, the mythology that gives power and credence to the new self and to the new social arrangements.

This symbolic universe may be very diverse, depending upon the nature of the identity and the complexity of the social arrangements. For the gang, the symbolic universe may offer a myth of a means of defending oneself and others from the violence that occurs in their neighborhoods, or a philosophy of life that offers the American dream through alternative means. For the ancient monk, the symbolic universe presented a rationale for a hierarchy of being in which the human ascends beyond the norm to become and live like an angel. For those at the gym, the world has been structured to include each athlete (if I can use that expression) as a perfect bodily specimen (despite the realities). This would include an anthropology and a particular theological understanding of the human condition as fallen and capable of restoration. The symbolic universe provides the deep structure, the meaning, the connectors, the rationale, the philosophy, and theology of the new subjectivity and its social relationships.

Essentially, an alternative identity with its different way of socializing should adjust the understanding of the world in which a person lives. Values and ethics change as the performance of the new identity is enacted. Ways of relating to others and to the physical environment shift as the new person comes into being. Connections between people and things, the bonds of everything in creation, transform as the new person emerges. All these ways of thinking constitute the symbolic universe in which the ascetic enacts a new identity.

Asceticism (as performances within a dominant social environment intended to inaugurate a new subjectivity, different social relations, and an alternative symbolic universe) then, addresses the larger question of how members of a society or community are trained to become particular kinds of people. Asceticism raises the larger question of cultural formation and reformation through a process of deconstructive withdrawal, constructive development and training, and fully empowered and articulated social identity in an altered understanding of the way the universe operates.

Modern Applications

I began studying asceticism intensively when I was chaplain to a religious order. My chaplain responsibilities included participating in the novitiate formation team consisting of the Novice Mistress, the Mother Superior, the

Assistant Superior, and a senior member of the order. Our task was to assist women in the early years of their religious life first to understand the religious life and its specific commitments, and second to assist them to discern their own place in the church as regarded this particular religious order or any other vocation in the church if she did not understand herself to be called to the religious life. Over the course of ten years, I encountered many women struggling with their religious vocations.

In working with this religious order, I observed that the senior members of the community (some women in life profession for fifty years or more, and most of them having accomplished many years of important urban ministry) had actively constructed a different way of living. They were capable of happily enduring the most difficult physical circumstances—as, for example, in the dangerous mission they had in Port-au-Prince, Haiti—and would, with deep devotion and sincere spirituality, conduct their ministry. How did these sisters come to be so happy doing their ministry under such difficult situations in the drug-infested sections of New York City, in the politically volatile and economically deprived missions of Haiti, among the very poor in upstate New York? They had clearly learned a different way of living. They practiced their particular form of religious life with the support of sisters practicing the same life.

The novices who learned this particular way of living experienced this as an affirmation of their vocation, and they tended to stay in the religious order. These novices grasped that they were living a life in another symbolic universe where the practices and performances had particular meaning. Once these novices grasped this system, then they could learn the specific performances to enact the way of life with grace and power.

However, the novices motivated by a desire to do ministry, by a calling to missionary endeavor, or by a need to be part of an intentional community tended to leave the order, neither affirming their vocation to the religious life, nor experiencing the grace for ministry that they had received prior to entering the novitiate of the order. This surprised me. On the surface, the people entering the religious order with a similar set of interests and missionary foci would seem to be the more likely to succeed and to remain, but they were not. It was only those who could see the different way of living, the different identity, the unique perspective of a monastic identity, who experienced a vocation and who ultimately could perform the most prophetic of ministries.

I began to study the manner in which unique monastic subjectivity was developed. I observed the ways in which the sisters became different people empowered for ministry; empowered to live in community; empowered to live in poverty, chastity, and obedience. After observing, we began to find particular ways of showing that new identity, those specific performances, those unique ways of relating in silence and solitude to other women, those unusual ways of understanding the world and the church from the perspective of a Bride of Christ. And in this, my study of asceticism was begun, and the contours of my theory developed.

What this experience as a monastic chaplain taught me was that people change or grow from "malleable bits of experience" into new kinds of people. Ideas do not change people; experiences change people, and the available base of experience needs carefully to be considered in the modern period. In order to begin to address the postmodern American situation, Americans need to envision concretely what kind of people we intend to be. I say concretely because we must envision our lives not at the level of ideology or of the ideal, but at the practical level, the performative level. How are we to relate to people who differ from us? How are we to treat people whose lives do not reflect our values? How do we have a cup of coffee with someone who hates our religious convictions? How do we live next door to people who lead a life totally at odds with ours? At the level of the ideal, we ignore the practical points of our lives and we embrace a kind of numbing perfectionism that defies actual living. So we must turn to the performative level to define precisely what actions we as a people intend to perform in order to create a new society or a new identity. We should be spending time revisioning the human state and its concrete and malleable basic units of experience so that we can project workable models and invite people to explore them.

My emphasis on performances demands that we answer questions that the public debate refuses to answer. Take the question of abortion. What will we do with the children we have saved from being aborted? Who will raise them? Who will provide a loving family environment for them? Who will pay for their education? Simply to make the theological or political statement that condemns abortion does not yet project an image, a model, or an achievable option to people in their lives. Breaking down the issue into "malleable bits" of experience will provide new directions for dealing with a serious and important issue.

This same procedure needs to be applied to moral formation generally. How do we form women and men in their decisions about their lives? Do we restrict their options, or do we engage with their lives and their problems in order to activate a different model for living? The proclamation that something is wrong works only at the ideological level without providing a concrete way for people to move beyond their current way of living into another modality. Moral decision making, and constructing moral decisions, does not happen only in the mind: morality involves a process of envisioning a new way of living and being equipped to move in those directions. But recognize that not all people will embrace the same system of morals, yet we will still need to be able to live with one another in local, national, and global communities.

These same "malleable bits of experience" also apply to what I consider a most critical conflict in current debate: a conflict between moral responsibility and fiscal relationships. It relates to the status and presence of the poor. The media and the government have systematically caricatured the poor (whether working poor, unemployed, or elderly) as a faceless and anonymous group without social or political value. Given that so many are characterized this way, a significant number of Americans believe that the poor may be dismissed. Poor people should not be constructed as a subjectivity that is metaphorized as an illness, or a siphon, or a virus on the corporate body in which we live. Somehow we must envision a kind of corporate identity that enables us to support and assist those weak members so that we support them in their need without patronizing them, so that we empower them to live as fully competent participants in the corporate body. This topic raises very concrete questions: How do we as a nation expect the poor to live? How do we envision the elderly to pay for medical insurance and prescriptions? How do we perform our honoring of the poor and the elders of our communities? What do we envision to be the set of social relationships that connect every member of our society into a common body? How do I live with the homeless people in my neighborhood? How can I relate to the elders in my community who need my support to be able to live (or to get medical attention)? At the performative level these questions look very different; they no longer allow me the option of looking only toward my beliefs, my thoughts, my understanding, my prejudices and they force me to look concretely at the lived experience of being a member of a community.

Church history has long proven that a return to past moral and ecclesiastical structures cannot be imposed. The rich and varied diversity of the early church has been repeated over and over again, not only in the Protestant Reformation and Catholic Reform, but also in the wild proliferation of Christian denominations and sects here in the United States. Christians cannot impose conformity; they must learn to live together with the diversity that has marked the Body of Christ since probably before Paul's missionary activity.

In this rich diversity, I return to the image of the gangs in my neighborhood. How can I live with them? I obviously cannot hold up to them a manner of living that they will embrace. I obviously cannot force them to obey the laws that connect us in civil relationship. I cannot convince them to put down their arms, to cease killing other children, to stop using drugs, to stop robbing merchants. I cannot control them. They live in another world from the one I live in; they have a different set of values than I have. Yet, they are part of the common life that we all share. We are still one body with them in society. Although people like me are dominant in the society, gangs cannot be thrown in jail, sequestered into walled ghettos and forgotten, shipped off to another city and allowed to kill themselves off. We must learn to live together, and yet the paucity of images, metaphors, ideal figures, or models, makes it difficult to imagine how we can cohere in one society. Our common life lacks the direction and definition that calls us each out to a form of asceticism that enables us to live together in harmony and peace, without violence and without imposing one regime on another. We simply do not know how to implement what we cannot imagine.

This dark view of the postmodern situation also sets the stage for a new direction. Rather than spending time imposing our will on others (however righteous we understand our will, knowing that others do not find it particularly righteous no matter what it is), we need to spend some time imagining what kind of characters we wish to become on the stage of postmodern American and global society and in the church. The goal of our human living should be developed not ideally, but with specific reference to the kind of performances, the malleable bits of experience and actions, in the concrete relationships necessary to develop that goal. It is an asceticism, a process of imagining a new way of living, a different kind of personality and identity, a consequent set of social relationships that supports that new vision, and creatively constructing the systems both intellectual and practical that will support it. The conflict we experience in our common life and in the church ought to encourage us all to the sort of withdrawal from the conflict that will enable us all to live together in new and vital ways.

Corporate Spiritual Formation

The asceticism of corporate spiritual formation operates at two interdependent levels: the personal and the corporate. The personal and corporate dimensions are interdependent because the performances that lead to a new identity, to a new way of operating in the world, must be performed by an individual in social and corporate contexts. Likewise, the corporate formation that takes place in assembled groups must manifest itself in the real lives of the individuals who make up the group. Both individual formation and community formation rely upon each other for support and for transformation. But each of these interdependent levels will depend upon specific performances to enact their new identity as a person and as a community.

Personal and corporate formation begins with a process of envisioning. As a person, each person must ask himself some questions: What kind of person do I want to be? What about my current way of living and being dissatisfies me? What do I need to change? Where am I headed as a person? These sorts of questions begin the process of envisioning the new identity, the new way of being and living, that forms the goal toward which the person moves. This vision of new being then raises the issue of the performances necessary to enact that new being and new way of living.

At the corporate level again there is a process of envisioning. To the community the process of envisioning asks similar questions: What sort of community do we want to be? What are our values and our orientations that satisfy us? What in our corporate lives dissatisfies us and makes us want to change? What do we want people who worship with us to experience through our corporate worship? What kinds of commitment do we expect from members of our community? How do we help people to live into those commitments? These and similar questions begin to form a vision of what the community wishes to become, of where the community is headed, and of how the members of the community will relate to one another. The vision (or visions) that follow from this process then raise the question of the specific performances that will enact that new community life and that new way of living together.

So for both individuals and communities, the beginning of asceticism is the goal (or goals) toward which the person works. The goal consists of visions of new life, new identity, and new ways of relating to one another and to the world. The instruments for achieving that goal (or those goals) is the specific performances that enact them and enable people and communities to be transformed. It is to the manner of such performances that we turn in the next chapter.

6

Performing New Life

THROUGH THE PREVIOUS CHAPTERS we have explored a number of analytical tools for studying community life. We began with the issue of creating a theological culture that will enable and empower people to live theologically in the midst of competing cultures. We explored a theory of communication that spotlighted the process of communication and identified some pitfalls when communication does not occur. We proposed an anthropology of three bodies (the physical, the social, and the corporate) as a lens through which to understand the complexities of human relationship in community. We explored narrative theory as a means of constructing community identity, and considered the process of creating a distinct language to enrich the community's life and communication. We analyzed the relationship of power and solidarity in the liturgical life of the community with special attention to the grammar, style, and accents of community life received from larger institutions and articulated in the local community's particular accent. And finally, we explored a theory of asceticism as a means of locating community formation in particular practices.

With all of these analytical tools still in mind, this chapter builds on the theory of asceticism to explore the way specific performances in community forms and enriches community life. The specific performances for each community will follow from the envisioning process so that the performances ought to be developed with specific goals in mind. The performances presented here, therefore, are merely examples of the manner in which a community might work toward their own goals. These performances, that is, are not proscriptive, but descriptive. The goals of each community will differ according to the specific proposed personality of the community and the kind of identity the community wishes to develop, but the processes are similar as each community works toward the transformation desired. I will present a few different scenarios and discuss the way in which the analytical tools have been addressed in the formative system put into place.

A Coffee-Hour Scenario

Let me begin with a very common and basic example. The parish my wife and I attended had a terrible coffee hour. Well it was not that the coffee was bad (although often it was), or that the coffee hour food was inedible (although often just a box of doughnut holes). The coffee hour was terrible because when we arrived as new members of the community, no one spoke to us. Our status as outsiders was underscored by the fact that all the people in the room knew each other and spent the coffee hour catching up with each other. No one spoke to us. We would often have a quick cup of coffee and run to the door to go home. The ministry of hospitality failed.

As the parish was growing in numbers and as we got to know more people, a member of the vestry approached my wife, Janet, to solve the coffee hour problem. The goal was that the ministry of hospitality after worship would provide new people with an opportunity to meet and talk with other members of the community and at the same time would provide a hospitable time for friends to gather and catch up. This was no small task.

So Janet set out to establish a host for each Sunday's coffee hour. Each Sunday she would bring her scheduling list and sign up hosts weeks in advance. Each host was given a set of guidelines to help them host the coffee hour. These guidelines included such things as setting a table with flowers or a centerpiece, arranging food on platters (even if the food was purchased from the grocery store), setting out coffee cups, providing condiments for the coffee, and generally treating the coffee hour as though this were to take place in the host's home. Those instructions related to the physical provision and arrangement of food and drink for the coffee hour. Janet also made clear that the primary ministerial function of the host was to attend to the visiting people and newcomers to the community. The host was to seek out the new people and visitors, talk with them, introduce them to other members of the parish, and then take them to the minister so that the minister could meet and greet them. Janet created a complete and specific system of performances for the host to lead to the transformation of the coffee hour.

The coffee hours became a huge success! Worshipers would come to the coffee hour and were greeted by a beautifully set table. The beauty of the table made even prosaic food taste good. Even the same coffee somehow tasted better. But more important, the communion that the worshipers experienced in the liturgy was carried through to communion experienced in another way in the coffee hour. The care taken to provide hospitality enabled that communion to occur, just as the care taken to provide good liturgy, preaching, and music had enabled spiritual communion to occur in the sanctuary. The specific coffee hour performances of the host transformed the experience of coming to the coffee hour.

The ministry of the hosts also took root. Someone was now in charge of attending to new people in order to greet them, make them feel truly welcomed and valued, and introduce them to other members of the community. The minister could spend time with new people, learn of their lives and interests, and begin to integrate them into the life of the community. And over the course of the year nearly fifty people engaged in the ministry of hospitality and were empowered to be hospitable throughout the year in the parish. As more and more people learned hospitality through being a host for a Sunday, the entire parish became more hospitable.

The coffee-hour ministry was an ascetical program. It trained many members of the parish in preparing a welcoming table. It also trained hosts to welcome new people and to integrate them into the ongoing life of the parish. Gradually it trained a major portion of the parish in hospitality. The coffee-hour ministry was a ministry of creating solidarity and of equalizing the power between new members and long-term members of the community. In performing the duties of coffee hour host, the process empowered people in the parish to take responsibility for the health and well-being of its members. Such attention to the details of a coffee hour, to the performance of hospitality, opened the space for the parish to grow and to thrive. Once members of the parish were hosts for a Sunday, they became regular ministers of hospitality throughout the year so that not only was the coffee hour transformed, but so that the entire parish culture was changed from exclusivity to hospitality.

A Complicated Liturgy

I know that the trend today is to make little booklets that include music and lessons so that people are not challenged to follow the liturgy. Some say this is easier for newcomers to the church. But let me argue for a decidedly different way of thinking about Sunday worship. The performance of a complicated liturgy creates solidarity within a parish.

I have spoken often of my experience at St. John's, Bowdoin Street, in Boston. It was a wonderful parish. The liturgy every Sunday was a solemn sung community Eucharist with excellent music, incense, chanting, and superb sermons. The parish had a long tradition of fine liturgical music and rich ceremonial. When we first attended, however, we were nonplussed. The greeter handed us a sheaf of papers: the music for congregational singing of the parts of the Eucharist, the lessons for the day, a sheet with the alleluias to be chanted before the gospel, a sheet with the plainsong psalm for the day, a bulletin, and a sheet of announcements of parish activities. These, together with the Hymnal and the Book of Common Prayer, were the tools necessary to participate in the community liturgy. We felt like we were carrying a library to the liturgy.

At first, it was very confusing for us. We knew the liturgy well from other parishes, but all these sheets of paper from this parish were overwhelming. As the liturgy began, however, and our look of confusion became evident, the person sitting in front of us turned around to us, showed us what we should be using from the sheaf of papers, and pointed to where we should be looking to participate. We smiled at each other, and giggled a little at our confusion. Obviously we needed to pay careful attention to each part of the Eucharist in order to be able to participate fully, and the sheaf of papers forced us to attend to where we were in the liturgy. At first we needed guides to help us through, and those guides became our companions in worship, even though we did not at first know them personally.

But over the course of time the liturgy transformed us. Each week as the liturgy unfolded slowly and majestically, we became more comfortable with the variable parts. We needed the guide less, but we still had to learn many things to be able to participate fully in the liturgy. Over time we learned many plainsong chant tones, and we mastered a number of different tones for the alleluia. The weekly liturgy was a time of training and spiritual formation so that over time we were experiencing the richness of the Christian and Anglo-Catholic tradition. As we learned more about chanting and singing, we became more adept at participating fully in this very complicated liturgy.

The complicated liturgy forced us to relate to other people in the congregation. At first, we needed others to guide us through the liturgy. Later, we became the guides to others. We experienced the other people participating in the liturgy as fellow wayfarers on the road to sanctification. We needed one another to be able to get through the liturgy. We supported one another as we learned to pray together. The complications in the liturgy became an important formative tool for creating solidarity among the congregation and for empowering each participant to pray attentively and with focus.

Through the discomfort of moving together from hymnal to liturgy book, of musical setting to plainsong chant, we were forming a corporate body that had deep ties in the liturgy and to the other participants in the liturgy. This is important. Our social bodies were being formed by our assistance to and support of one another in the liturgy. We were connecting deeply with people we did not know so that we might learn how to pray together. Our physical bodies were no longer isolated from one another in the pews; we were all in this together. So slowly over time, we were grafted on to the corporate body of the parish. We did not necessarily know these other people personally. We may not have known their work or their families, or their stories but we did pray together, learning to move together gracefully from book to book and paper to paper. The corporate body was being formed precisely because the liturgy was too complicated to be easily navigated, and because in order to get through the liturgy we needed one another's support and direction.

At the same time, however, we were forging a common language for corporate prayer. The psalm tones, which changed week by week, and the alleluia tones, which changed seasonally, became part of the specific accents of our prayer language. By mastering these ancient chant tones, we were developing a particular language for prayer for that community. The singing and chanting of these elements of the liturgy forced us as a corporate body to breathe together and to enter into a common voice of prayer. Our language, based in the ancient traditions, was brought to life week by week by our enacting a tradition much older than our parish itself. The language and chants of the tradition became alive again as we chanted them, and we gave them new articulation in the context of our own lives. The tradition in this way became not something of the past, but something we lived and experienced week by week in a startlingly different context.

Children in Church

I was raised in the Greek Orthodox Church. There has never been a time in my life, from my earliest childhood until now, that I have experienced the church as anything other than my second home. I recall being lifted to venerate the icons, lighting candles with my mother and great aunt, scurrying through the church playing, crying, and fussing during the services, and running around with my friends. I am sure it was chaos for everyone, but I was a part of the liturgy, even as I experienced it obliquely.

I have been watching my godson Paxton who has been part of our eucharistic community from the womb until now. During the liturgy he plays with his cars or with the tinker toys. He huddles under the altar table. He runs around, eats snacks, engages with the participants, and otherwise seems to live in his own play world. But when the gifts of bread and wine are brought to the altar, he says, "Time to eat." He knows, even though he is not participating as the adults, exactly what is going on during the liturgy. He enthusiastically exchanges the peace. Even more enthusiastically he blows out the candles on the altar at the end of the service. He notes everything that takes place in the liturgy, even though he seems not to be engaging.

At St. John's, Bowdoin Street, we set up a play area in the church for our children. The children were free to roam the church. Some would crawl up to the altar, others would find their way to the pulpit, still others would move about the pews, while others were playing in the aisles. At times it was chaos. We wanted, however, the children to experience the church as their place. We wanted them to be at home in the church as much as in their own homes or in their schools. The church was their home as well. We did not expect them to sit quietly, like the adults, knowing that it was nearly impossible for them to do so. We did not expect them to attend to the liturgy in the same way as the adults, but we wanted them to find their place in the liturgy, a place suitable to their age and needs.

At first, some adults were taken aback by the children's behavior. It is not that they did not love and appreciate the children, but that the children's behavior imposed on their participation in the liturgy. The adults needed to find a different way to participate in the liturgy—a way that included the children. We encouraged the adults to be forbearing: these are our children; this is their home too. Gradually over time everyone adjusted to the disruptions and activity, and everyone learned a different way to pray. At times the celebrant would have to engage with a child during the liturgy; at other times other people in the congregation would need to attend to a child's need. The children became a vital part of our liturgical experience. We learned to bear one another's burdens, becoming at one time or another a parental substitute for the child. We learned to concentrate on our participation in the liturgy in ways that accommodated the children and their play. Their play was, after all, their way of participating in the liturgy. Their play was prayer too. They too were experiencing in their own way the unfolding mystery of God's presence in that building.

By including the children in the liturgy and liturgical space, we were in the process of changing the culture of our parish. The received culture says that the liturgy, the time of worship, is for adults, and for adult ways of engaging and praying. This received culture stipulates that we send children off to church school during the service, because they cannot understand the liturgy in an adult way. The church school presumably engages with children in children's ways of knowing and praying. But by including the children, we opened our parish culture to new ways of praying, new ways of engaging with God, and different ways of being a community. Our parish culture said that the liturgy belongs to the people and is the people's work. Children, as members of the community, were entitled to participate in their own way with as much authority and acceptance that any adult would expect as a participant in the liturgy. Children, after all, were part of God's people as well.

The emerging culture also located worship more fully in our bodies. This is important. The received culture seems to locate the reality of worship in the attentive mind. We pay attention to the words and actions of the liturgy, and by paying attention we participate with our minds. But our parish culture suggested that true worship was with a body engaged, a soul connected to other souls in whatever age or state they existed, and a mind at once attentive to God and to the other people around us. To include the children in our social and corporate bodies was to expand the understanding of ourselves. The children's performance of their prayer during the liturgy forced us to change our culture and to be more inclusive of other ways of praying than with the mind alone.

This emerging culture also created a strong sense of solidarity between generations. The parents of the children could relax, because the church was full of parents willing to engage with their children during the liturgy. We parented not only one another's children but one another as well. We became a corporate body of parenting and support, which we experienced week after week as we engaged with the children growing up in our midst.

Moreover, we gave power to our children to pray and live with God in whatever way was appropriate to them. This too is important. By our actions—our performances during liturgy—we showed the children that there is a wide variety of ways of worshiping God, and we validated their own particular ways of participating (even when their way annoyed us!). We empowered the children to share in the experience of the liturgy, and to guide us into new ways of praying and living together.

A Discursive Community

At the height of the AIDS pandemic our parish went into full gear of ministry to those gay men who would come to us for ministration and support as they were dying. It was an intense time in the parish. Week after week, it seemed, young men would come to us for help and support, having been rejected by their families and their home churches who feared the disease that infected the young men and who despised the gay and lesbian way of living. Depressed and fearful, these young men would come to us for love and support. The parish responded fully. We provided them love and support, fed them, visited them in the hospital, prayed for them, attended to the medical and spiritual needs of their ailing bodies, in the end prayed and held them in our arms as they died, and brought their bodies into the church to be buried. This scenario persisted for many months, and the parish ministrations were very taxing.

Jennifer Phillips and I, co-rectors of the parish, spent a great deal of time talking about the effect of this ministry on the parish. Our parish was a mixed parish of heterosexual and homosexual couples, of gay and lesbian and straight single people, of rich and poor, of professional and homeless, and of many people who had been deeply wounded in their lives. It was a vital and lively parish. The fear that we had as ministers was that the only recognition of gay and lesbian folks in the parish was around their wounds and hurts. We seemed to deal with gay and lesbian members of the parish only when they were in crisis or pain. The AIDS crisis only accentuated this reality. We were only dealing with the gay and lesbian members of our parish in the most drastic of circumstances. And we did not think this was healthy or spiritually beneficial. We had to celebrate gay and lesbian lives in the same way we celebrated heterosexual people's lives in the parish. We had to find a way to celebrate the whole person and people in holy relationships, whether homosexual or heterosexual.

Jennifer and I made a pastoral decision. It was time to celebrate the lives of every member of the community. With many gay and lesbian couples that wanted to get married (note: this was nearly thirty years ago!), we decided that we would start blessing and recognizing their relationships. We needed to celebrate gay and lesbian joys as well as sorrows. In a sermon on a Sunday, I announced that we would begin immediately to formulate a liturgy for the marriage (then we called it a covenanting) of gay and lesbian couples, and that we would use the same liturgy for the blessing and recognition of heterosexual couples.

Needless to say, this decision instantiated a disagreement with our bishop and with the leadership of the wider church. We began conversations within the parish to explore the riches and depth of our commitment to gay and lesbian members, to understand the significance of their relationships to all the heterosexual members of the congregation, and to strategize about how we might present our case to our bishop and to the church at large. These conversations were most decisive in the deepening of relationships among our congregants. We also invited the bishop and his staff to attend a parish meeting to discuss with us our need to recognize gay and lesbian couples, to bless their relationships, and openly to support them with all the fervor and grace with which we recognized and supported heterosexual relationships.

We planned a series of parish meetings to engage in these conversations and preparations for talking with the bishop. These meetings were intense. Couple after couple shared their stories. The gay and lesbian couples revealed the joy of their relationships, the pain of discovering their sexual orientation, the rejection they experienced from family and friends, the struggle to maintain a holy relationship in an often hostile environment, the joy of finding a parish that honored and respected and accepted them, the hurt they experienced from other parishes and the church at large, and the struggle to be holy and godly people among people who considered them a pariah. Heterosexual couples told their stories as well, telling the congregation of their lives and loves, of their deep relationship with gay and lesbian couples, of the similarity of stories between their lives and the lives of fellow parishioners, of their struggles as couples, and of their faith and life in the church. Over the course of these parish meetings, a significant portion of the parish grew to love and understand each other in ways that no other conversations could have provided. Those conversations were deep and intense and personal and revealing and very, very real experiences that cut to the heart.

We decided at our last meeting that when the bishop came to meet with us that the heterosexual couples would speak first so that the stories would be less threatening to the bishop and so that gay and lesbian couples were not put in the spotlight immediately. When the gay and lesbian couples felt safe in the conversation, they could then tell their stories.

The night of the meeting was a miserably rainy night, as only New England winters can have them. The parish hall was filled to capacity. We were all very nervous and anxious about how the evening would progress and what the outcome would be. The bishop arrived a little late. We prayed to open the evening, and then the conversation began. Because we had been telling each other our stories, the first couples that spoke were articulate and theological and scripturally based. They spoke with passion and love. Jennifer and I, who chose not to speak at all as the clergy, were very proud of them. Then the gay and lesbian couples began to speak. They too were passionate and theological and scripturally based. They spoke from the depth of their experience and from the riches of the Christian tradition to the shepherd of their diocese. The evening wore on as couple after couple stood up to talk to the bishop and the congregation. Tears flowed. Hearts were broken. Laughter and joy abounded. Lives were being changed before our eyes. The parish had never been so united, so articulate, so theological, and so deeply connected to the ancient traditions of the church.

At the end of the meeting, the bishop looked overwhelmed. He had never encountered so articulate and passionate a parish! He was in a dilemma. He too was deeply moved by the stories, but felt he was restrained by the larger church from accepting such relationships as truly Christian. He said this to the assembled congregation. We could hear him, but we stood firm: either we recognize the full lives of gay and lesbian people in the church, or we tell them to leave the church because they cannot receive the sacraments and ministrations of the church. We either accepted them fully as baptized members of the Body of Christ, or we send them away as unacceptable to be members of Christ. We could not baptize people and then reject them because of the way they loved; to do this would be to perpetuate abuse of people in the church. This was a firm theological belief of everyone in our parish. In the end, we proceeded with the blessing of gay and lesbian couples, and entered a time of deep division with our bishop and the Church.

I tell this story because it reveals the way language and discourse develop parish life. The crisis in our parish forced us to develop deep relationships with one another in order to perform the ministry to which God called us. We needed to find a language, a theology if you will, that would articulate for us clearly our deepest values and our unique Christian perspective. Our words about relationships and love needed to have the stories of the people so that when we spoke of relationship we remembered the stories of pain and joy of our parishioners. Our language, our discourse, needed to be enfleshed with real-life experiences, so that when we spoke to one another we spoke out of the depth of experience. This is what I have meant by the need to develop a language, to enter a deep discourse, so that words carry the deep connotations of real experience. Without the parish meetings and our meeting with the bishop, our language about love and relationship would have remained shallow and surface, but having related real and deep experiences, our language became vital, energized, and rich in meaning. When we spoke with one another, we heard the deep meaning of words, and we spoke with the richness of meaning of our words, because we knew the experiences that formed the language. Our language reflected the deep solidarity we experienced in telling our stories. Our language reflected the rich power that our theology gave us to stand up solidly before the church and the world to do the new things the Holy Spirit was directing. Our language and discourse took on a depth and richness not otherwise common in community life.

Moreover, our conversations in the parish developed a different culture. The symbolic universe in which we lived in our parish shifted to include gay and lesbian relationships and expanded our understanding of baptism and the sacraments. We discovered in these conversations that the work of the church was to create families, starting with gay and lesbian couples but extending to all sorts of relationships of love and mutual support. Our culture became one of deep caring and cherishing of one another without respect to sexual orientation or to social class. Our culture also became richly theological. We no longer lived according to the received values of the church, but based upon our reading of Scripture and our exploration of theology, we could move solidly in new directions without a sense of breaking with the past, but rather with a sense of doing what the Spirit was guiding us to do, despite opposition from others.

So much of the time, we do not really know the people with whom we worship on a Sunday or with whom we share life in a parish. Meeting casually on a Sunday and going to a coffee hour, we maintain relationships and language that operate mostly on the surface. To take time to develop a deep language with one another demands that we practice telling the narrative of our lives to others without fear or shame. Without that rich discourse and language, our relationships remain vapid; but with rich discourse and language, forged in the deep conversations about our lives, our relationships grow deep and become more transformative. It is this development of language that leads the way to depth.

A Sundance Model

I participate in the High Star Sun Eagle International Sundance for Peace in Red Valley, Arizona. I have participated for a number of years, having completed my four-year commitment a few years ago. A four-year commitment is required in order to complete a cycle of prayer for each sacred direction (North, South, East, and West) and in order to complete a cycle of personal prayer and intention for dancing. The sundance, whose intercessor is Howard Bad Hand (Lakota), brings together Native Americans from a number of different tribes to dance for peace among people and in the world. The sundance consists of four days of purification and four days of dancing: eight days in total.

During the purification time, a number of things happen. The primary function is that the dancers have time each day to enter a sweat lodge. In this lodge, the dancers share their intention for prayer during the dance and learn of other dancers' intentions so that the dancers may support one another's prayer in the dance. It is a time of deep intimacy and often of sharing difficult life circumstances that challenge and that lead one to pray intensely during the dance. In the sweat lodge, the dancers form strong bonds of mutual support in prayer and in living.

Also during the purification time there are many mundane tasks that must be completed. The sundance arbor must be cleaned and prepared for use. The rest area for the dancers must be cleaned and shaded. Firewood for the sacred fire must be cut. Stones for the sweat lodges must be gathered from the mountains. Cedar for smudging during the dance must be gathered and cut. The dancers need to prepare sage crowns, bracelets, and anklets to wear during the dance. A road to the tree, which stands at the center of the arbor and around which the dancers dance, must be made. Dancers and supporters must set up their camps for sleep. The kitchen must be cleaned and prepared for cooking for supporters and dancers. Food must be purchased; supplies for the week must be procured. Sweat lodges must be covered with tarps. A myriad of tasks must be accomplished in just four short days. These are challenging tasks and difficult work. It is a flurry of communal activity that takes place in the context of each dancer's intention to pray. The community, a group of people who only see each other at the sundance, learns to live and work together in harmony and peace as they prepare for the dance. These mundane tasks force the participants to learn to live and work in harmony.

On tree day, which marks the turning point between purification and dance, the community gathers at the tree selected the year before, to pray with it, to thank it for the life it is giving so that the people may pray and flourish, and to carry it ceremonially into the arbor. Once the tree is brought into the arbor and before it is set up in the center, dancers and supporters and singers put their prayer ties and prayer flags on it. These prayer ties and flags represent the prayers and intentions of all the people, which the tree holds up to the sky during the dance. Once the tree is set up in the arbor, the arbor becomes a sacred place, and there follows a feast in celebration of the beginning of the dance. Once the tree is set up, the dancers must not have any contact with water.

The dance days begin very early in the morning, before the sun rises. The dancers come to the dance arbor to prepare. They may not eat or drink water or touch water for the four days of the dance, although some may eat a little at night to keep up their strength. Each morning the dancers begin the day with a round of prayer and song in the sweat lodge. Then they dress in their dance vesture and put on their sage crowns, bracelets, and anklets. They prepare their pipes with prayer and tobacco. As the sun is rising, the dancers enter the arbor praying to each direction (North, South, East, and West) as they process to the entry gate. In the first round of dancing, the entry round, the dancers bring their pipes to the tree and pray. There are generally eight rounds in the sundance: the entrance and exit with six rounds intervening. We have danced in snow, blistering heat, sandstorms, rainstorms, and in every possible weather condition in-between. The days are long and challenging. The prayer is palpable. At the end of each dance round, a group of pipes is given out to the supporters, until at the end of the day all the pipes have been distributed and shared with the supporters as a means of including them in the prayers of the dance.

In the time between rounds, the dancers rest in their rest area. There is a great deal of jovial conversation and teasing, as well as times of serious talk about matters of concern. The dancers support one another, encouraging one another to persist. Of course, there are also naps and quiet time. The aim is to help one another to dance their prayers, as Howard Bad Hand describes it. Often between rounds of dancing, there are also special prayers for healing, for celebrating life events, and for recognizing the accomplishments and gifts of people living and dead. The day is a full day, ending usually close to sundown.

The prayer is powerful through these four days of dancing. People are healed. Others are transformed. Lives are changed in many ways. Those who have participated either as dancers or as supporters find themselves to be different people at the end of the dance. The dance for peace has indeed brought harmony and peace into the lives of the individuals and into the lives of the assembled community.

I describe the sundance experience because it reveals how necessary it is to take on the ascetical disciplines for common worship. So much of our Western worship is something that we simply take for granted. We do not prepare for it. We do not expect to work or exert effort while we are worshiping. The sundance points to another reality: worship demands preparation, sincere and articulated intention, and demanding effort. Our liturgies are our sundance. Readers should be studying the lessons all week to prepare to give a good and substantial public reading during the liturgy. There should be rehearsals, so that the movements of the liturgy are graceful and intentional. The choir, accustomed to such preparation, should be ready to sing the prayers of the people (as opposed to performing for them). The people who gather for worship must be prepared to pray, to engage, to expect new revelations from God about their lives and commitments. In other words, liturgy is hard work, and it should be hard work. Liturgy should always challenge and demand.

In former times, the weekly liturgy, especially the Eucharist, demanded preparation. One had to go to private confession before receiving the sacrament. One fasted from food and water before receiving. One might ask the forgiveness of those with whom they lived to clear the path for renewal. Now these disciplines have been forgotten, and as a result our liturgies have lost their power. I am not arguing for a return to the disciplines of former times but for a sense of discipline around public worship. Our disciplines may be different: an asceticism of study, a list of particular intercessions, a reflection on the week to acknowledge areas of our lives in need of reformation and renewal, an offering of food for the hungry and homeless, or any other instrument we might develop individually and corporately to demand that we prepare for our weekly public worship. The sundance succeeds precisely because of the participants' intent, their hard work, their endurance of harsh circumstances, and their joyful dancing of their prayers.

The asceticism of liturgical participation builds community. The preparation in advance of the liturgy provides an opportunity to focus attention and intention, while at the same time investing liturgy with power and authority. By preparing for liturgy, we empower the liturgy to be an agent of transformation in our lives. We also, at the same time, create deep solidarity with other members of the community (and with God) by hearing one another's specific intercessions, by celebrating life's events together, by mourning together, and by engaging in the deep theological discourse that our preparation has made possible for us. This deep and transforming liturgy is not found in the words of the liturgy but in the real preparation of the people who are participating in it.

Assembling the Bodies

A clergy colleague has a spectacular way of celebrating All Saints Day. She invites the members of her congregation to bring in icons of their favorite saints from the past and pictures of those living and dead saints who have had a significant part in their lives. These icons and pictures are placed throughout the church on the walls, and a table of pictures and icons stands at the front near the altar.

Walking into the church on All Saints Sunday is a walk into the social body of the parish, the corporate body. We see icons of saints and angels, pictures of grandparents, parents, aunts, uncles, teachers, friends, and companions. We experience the social body of the church at large, as well as the social body of the members of the parish. We are all gathered into one space, praying together with saints and angels, with loved ones, and with the people living and dead who have made us who we are. The sense of the community of faith, of the endless witnesses to the faith, old and new, becomes palpable upon entering the church. And the liturgy becomes resplendent with the presences of our social and corporate bodies.

The sense of not being an isolated individual is an important one. Each of us comes to community life and to worship with many people within us who have had a significant impact on our lives. We are never alone. We are never isolated. Some of those who are a part of our social bodies are people who have hurt us. These destructive ones also make us who we are. Some of those who are part of our social bodies are people who have been our guides, our support, our lovers, and our inspiration. These wonderful people also have made us who we are. And God is always present within us, not distant and far away but alive and working within us in mysterious and often hidden ways. We have a social body that we bring to the corporate body.

Taking our various bodies seriously enriches our spiritual life. We live because they lived. We thrive because they have been a part of our lives, for good or ill. We grow in faith and in love, because they are a part of who we are. When we gather the bodies for prayer or worship or discourse, we manifest the reality of our communal being. At times we remember parts of our social bodies in the intercessions; at other times we remember them during the offering; at still other times we struggle with them during the liturgy for the harm they have done to us; and then we give thanks for their lives and for the path they have guided us on. Just as we view a host of icons and pictures on All Saints Sunday, so we live with a host of others who live within us, and we pray with them, and we honor them for their witness. We are never alone, either in worship or in prayer; we are always connected to a host of others who still live within us.

When we gather and pray with all our bodies (physical, social, and corporate) gathered, we begin to experience the richness and depth of our connections to the past and to the present. We bring along with us those who have died and had an influence on our lives, and we introduce those members of our social bodies to others in our corporate bodies so that all of them participate in the liturgy along with us. The bodies become rich and teeming with presences that enhance and energize our worship. And we have the experience of never being totally alone, because we bear these presences in our bodies.

Making the Bodies Dazzle

These examples have intended to spur your imagination. They are not prescriptions of the way the spiritual life of individuals or communities are formed, but rather examples of how the religious life might be lived with authenticity and dignity. Throughout this book, I have focused on analyzing experiences and providing theoretical frames for that analysis. The emphasis has been on the investigation of real-life experiences and on tracing the associations in those experiences that lead to fullness of life. These experiences make the body dazzling—whether the physical body, the social body, or the corporate body. The dazzling body is the one that is truly alive to the self, to others, to the physical universe in which we live, and to the divine presence that pervades all reality.

I must be clear. The theories presented here are not objective. I do not think that we can be completely divorced from the realities of our lives as we investigate them. We cannot be objective. But the theories come to experiences in personal and communal life from another dimension. The theories allow us to look at our experiences in community through lenses that open these experiences to investigation, reflection, and reform. Often our community life as well as our personal lives seem opaque and difficult to understand. This is natural. We live life, and then we reflect on it, while often not understanding the personal and corporate dynamics at work in our actions. These theories afford us the opportunity to investigate and reflect with various means in order to open our experiences to reflection and to open paths for transformation and renewal in our daily lives alone and together.

It has been the argument of this book that spirituality has more to do with reflection on practice than on a way of thinking. This is important to note. I do not disparage the work of the mind in thinking and meditating. That is not my goal. Rather my goal has been to relocate the center of spirituality from the personal and intellectual to the practical and the performative, and to locate the spiritual life in a reflective practice on the performance. It is in this reflective practice on the realities of daily living that the spiritual life becomes vital and real. It is in this reflective practice that the bodies become dazzling.

Formation takes place in this reflective practice. When we reflect on the real-life experiences of our daily living alone and together, we experience the dissatisfaction with the way we live and begin to work toward transformation and renewal. In that dissatisfaction, we begin the ascetical struggle to make ourselves new people and to remake our communities and world to reflect the new life we desire. In that reflective practice, we look at the goal of who we want to be and in what kind of community we want to live, and we dream up practices and performances that will lead us into fullness of life. In setting forth practices and performances, we begin immediately to enact that new person, to create that new community, and to dazzle in the fullness of life that comes from our practices.

One of the most significant shifts in the symbolic universe that takes place by a focus on performance and practice is in the realm of what is real. Practices take place in the physical realm, in the world of real-life experience. We quite naturally assume that what we do is indeed real. Often, however, when we discuss spiritual matters, matters of faith, we revert to thinking that these realities are mostly symbolic. We distance the real from the spiritual by consigning the spiritual to merely symbolic action. We think of our participation in the Eucharist, for example, as a symbolic or figurative union with God rather than as an actually real and tangible union with God through the eating of the Bread of Heaven and the drinking of the Cup of Salvation. But these actions are not symbolic or figurative; these actions are real union: they are just as real as giving a sandwich to a hungry person or giving a coat to one who is homeless. By focusing on the practice and the performances, we infuse the physical world with the reality of the presence of God. The God, who is ever present with us in the church and in the world, acts and lives through our actions and practices. God is not distant but immanent in our daily activities. We enter that reality of God in our performances of the spiritual life in the physical realm. So the practices, the performances, make God present in the real world in which we live. If we think of our practices figuratively, we distance that immediate reality. The emerging new symbolic universe is one in which the reality of God is made visible and tangible in the actions and performances of our daily lives. This is an important shift in understanding, and one that follows naturally from our practices of the spiritual life.

The practices and performances form the person and the community in the real world—that is, in the world in which God is present and evident in the actions of the person and the community. We know who we are by what we do, not just by what we think. Our actions express our spirituality, so the formation we seek is through enacting our spiritual reality in practices that reveal the divine presence. So formation occurs through continued reflection on the significance and efficacy of our actions, our practices, our performances. Too often a divide emerges between (on the one hand) who we think we are, and what we believe, and (on the other hand) what we actually do, how we actually relate to other people and the physical universe in which we live, and what our actions actually mean. Thinking and reflection (theology, if you will) follows from the activities and performances of the various bodies (of the physical body, the social body, and corporate body). In a sense we do not conform our bodies to a way of thought and belief, but we reflect on the reality of our actions to inform ourselves of our real and functional theology. If we are dissatisfied with the theological implication of our actions and practices, then we must begin to reform our practice in order to change our theology.

The tools presented in this book assist us in that process of reformation and renewal. These tools create a space in which reflection on action may occur. In this analytical space, we may interrogate our actions and practices and relationships in order to forge a vision of the new person and new community we desire to see enacted. With these tools we can examine the old self and the old community and can begin to forge a vision of the new, while envisioning the practices through whose enactment that new reality may come into existence and be real and tangible.

When we put our parish and community life of liturgy and service under the microscope of theories of analysis, we begin to see the reality of the blessings and failings of community. The same applies to our personal lives. We discover the cultures in which we live, and we attempt to develop the culture that makes our bodies dazzle and our lives full. Granted, there are competing cultures all around us, but we may enact the culture and live the culture that brings most life and vitality. We can learn to communicate deeply and truly the signs and articulations that bring life and health to us and to our communities. Our bodies—the physical, the social, and the corporate—may become resplendent with the presence of God in them, and our bodies will shine with the glory of that divine presence. We will be able to tell our personal and corporate stories in such a way that the narratives will glisten with divine light, forging a language characterized by vitality, depth, and sincerity. When we interrogate ourselves and our communities, we will see the systems of solidarity in which we live, and so we will express the proper relationships to power. And when we enter into the ascetical transformation through our performances and practices, we will see the new person and the new life emerging in a symbolic universe in which what we believe becomes real and tangible in our actions for others.

This is the vision of the dazzling bodies that I have attempted to describe in this book. The vision is not so far off that we cannot achieve it, but the vision's transformation demands analysis and reflection as well as reformation of practices. Dazzling bodies are well worth the effort.

Afterword

By this point in this book, you have figured out that I am of Greek heritage and that I was reared in the Greek Orthodox Church. It is odd because at the writing of this book I have been an Episcopal priest longer than I was an Orthodox layperson. The roots of spiritual formation run very deep and often can be changed only with intentional and prolonged activity. In the end I have not changed all that much. I am probably still simply an Anglo-Orthodox or an Eastern Rite Anglican or some hybrid such as this. At the same time, I can say that I have been completely transformed by my Episcopal life in that I no longer experience God and the world through the lenses provided for me by my Orthodox childhood. The interaction of formation systems has produced in me something new and something very old at the same time.

As an Orthodox child I did not remember a time when I was not a part of my parish's liturgy. I do not remember a time when I did not receive Communion, the Body and Blood of Jesus, as a means of sanctifying my life. Receiving Communion is a lifelong memory. There was no time when I could not remember the sound of Byzantine chant, the smell of incense mixed with burning beeswax candles, the glitter of icons with olive-oil lamps burning in front of them, the fading light of evening while Vespers were being chanted, the long hours of standing at all sorts of liturgies. These experiences formed who I was. I brought those experiences with me to the Episcopal Church. I brought the value of actively involving children in the liturgy, of making liturgy appeal to the senses, of thinking liturgically about parish life, of making theology out of community activity, of focusing the mind fully on God in the midst of a vital community, of having a God living and true and accessible to me and to my Episcopal parishes. The incorporation of these values and practices into my Episcopal life, however, was not simply a grafting, but a transformation. I brought experience of liturgy and community life that had deep and abiding roots, and those experiences were transformed, translated, and reformed in the context of my Episcopal parishes. The language of the *Book of Common Prayer* formed my language, the structure of the liturgy became the primary means of worship, the kind of community life and parish structure provided the context for my intellectual and spiritual growth and maturation. I entered a different world, a world in which I put down deep Protestant and Catholic roots on a transplanted Orthodox and Eastern Christian plant. Formation is an important factor in modern church life precisely because it enables the transformation of self in specific contexts.

I was called, of course, a wild Byzantine in the Episcopal Church. It is a title I bear with honor, because what I brought with me was really a distant part of Episcopal, and even more broadly, of Christian life. In the early church, especially after the establishment of Christianity by Constantine the Great in the fourth century, community formation happened during the intense and prolonged preparation for baptism. The early church understood that a person needed to be trained to be able to live the Christian life. Somewhere along the line, Christians have forgotten that message. By the time we get to formation, it is too late.

I started this book in Denver, Colorado. In the wake of the mass killing of students at Columbine High School in April, 1999, many people have talked about the need to change the way people treat one another. Since then there have been many more tragic shootings: Virginia Tech, Sandy Hook, Aurora, among others. It is a public conversation, which takes place in newspapers, on the television, in magazines, on the radio, in schools, in churches, in classrooms, in government halls. But it is a conversation that lacks direction and depth. One state legislator thought that the simply posting the Ten Commandments on the wall of every classroom in the state would form students to be different sorts of people: less violent, more respectful and God-fearing, and better equipped to live together in harmony. The legislator is correct in his appraisal, but we all seem to lack the proper skills for assessing and addressing that need.

Dazzling Bodies envisions an articulate means of assessing the state of health of a community through a reading of its common activities. Formation begins with the realization that we are all connected. I underscore the realization of human interconnectedness because I think that the fact of our connections one to another cannot be disputed. I have tried to set forth some categories for utilizing that realization by metaphorizing the religious world of a local community when it gathers as a culture, and by describing people's various bodies and the way they interrelate in a corporate setting. When we begin to make our connections visible and when we begin to take seriously our interrelationships as a significant part of living, then we will be embarking on corporate spiritual formation. The process begins when we understand that no one of us is isolated from another and that through the social bodies of others, each of us connects to innumerable people whom we do not know. The network of interconnection stands wide and deep.

After realizing that we are interconnected, we can then begin to work those relationships for our common good. There is a rich fabric to human existence being woven of diverse threads. It is not a finished weaving, but one in progress. We weave that fabric, continuing the weaving begun centuries ago, and adding to a weaving that will continue forever. God, through the incarnation of Jesus Christ, wove God's own self into the process, ultimately connecting each one of us not only to each other but to the All-gracious God as well. Our human efforts at spiritual formation determine the quality of that weaving in our own times. We can make a difference, not because God is not present and because it is all our own effort, but precisely because God is present and can make all things new, dazzling, and resonant. The realization of the interconnected reality of human existence before God starts us weaving so that we realize our connections to the past and our bridging to the future.

It is not an accident that the Bible starts with God's speaking words in the creation to call all things into existence. It is also no accident that the Gospel of John images Jesus as the Word that was spoken and that has taken on human flesh to dwell among us. Words are important. The language we use with one another and with God defines who we are and how we relate. The deeply divisive language of racism and heterosexism, to say nothing of homophobia and xenophobia, are words that deeply wound, even when simply spoken. Words have power. Finding and developing language for articulating our highest aspirations as humans and as religious people becomes an important part of constructing our identity. Language enables us to graft many different people into our social bodies, even people we do not know personally, even people who cause us problems, even people with whom we would not normally associate. The words we use not only mirror who we are at this time, but they also point to who we want to become in the future. Words are central to the process of human and religious formation.

Words also function as signs in a process of communication. Words are powerful, but they become effective in communication. The ability to transform society depends upon communication. We communicate in a variety of different ways. Intentionally, we communicate when we begin to speak to another person or to God. But such intentionality does not exhaust the communicative process. We also communicate through other signs: through gesture, clothing, seating, repetition of common prayers, singing, facial expressions, bodily posture; this list could go on forever. We humans are communicative beings by nature and we communicate continually, even when we are not in direct conversation with people, but simply through our normal activities in the world. Corporate spiritual formation involves the transformation of our communication systems so that what we communicate by our verbal and gestural activities—our seating, our speaking, our gestures, our songs, our meetings, our liturgies—expresses the values we hold dear. This alignment of intention with corporate activity (should I simply call this alignment a theological perspective?) stands at the heart of corporate formation. When we communicate to a child that the community truly values her participation by including her in the liturgy, then the child experiences that value in words and in action. If we say we are a parish that values children and then push them off away from the main activity of the parish at worship, then children receive a mixed message, one that ultimately will subvert the experience of inclusion. Communication follows the sense of connectedness and the development of language in the process of corporate spiritual formation.

In the end, the entire process is an ascetical one. Our asceticism projects a new kind of person in a new set of relationships, and in a newly conceived world, which begins to be enacted in specific and articulated performances. These performances make our bodies dazzle, and that is the most important kind of life we may live. Writing this book has been just such an ascetical enterprise for me. I have relived and interrogated many very important experiences both personal and corporate in these pages. These experiences came to life again in my body, and with my reflecting on them in writing this book, my bodies became resplendent with the theological reality of the divine presence. I pray the same for you in your analysis and reading.

Bibliography

Barthes, Roland. *Mythologies*. Translated by Annette Lavers. New York: Noonday, 1992.
————. *The Rustle of Language*. Translated by Richard Howard. New York: Hill & Wang, 1986.
Bellah, Robert, et al. *Habits of the Heart: Individualism and Commitment in American Life*. Berkeley: University of California Press, 1985.
Bouyer, Louis, et al. *History of Christian Spirituality*. Translated by Mary P. Ryan. 3 vols. New York: Seabury, 1963.
Cousins, Ewert, ed. *World Spirituality: An Encyclopedic History of the Religious Quest*. New York: Crossroads, 1986.
Douglas, Mary. *Purity and Danger: An Analysis of the Concepts of Pollution and Taboo*. London: Routledge, 1966.
Eco, Umberto. *A Theory of Semiotics*. Advances in Semiotics. Bloomington: Indiana University Press, 1979.
Geertz, Clifford. *The Interpretation of Cultures: Selected Essays*. New York: Basic Books, 1973.
Haraway, Donna, "The Biopolitics of Postmodern Bodies: Determinations of Self in Immune System Discourse." *Differences: A Journal of Feminist Cultural Studies* 1/1 (1989) 3–43.
Hodge, Robert, and Gunther Kress. *Social Semiotics*. Ithaca: Cornell University Press, 1988.
Innis, Robert E, ed. *Semiotics: An Introductory Anthology*. Bloomington: Indiana University Press, 1985.
Jones, Cheslyn, et al., eds. *The Study of Spirituality*. New York: Oxford University Press, 1986.
Lakoff, George, and Mark Johnson. *Metaphors We Live By*. Chicago: University of Chicago Press, 1980.
Malina, Bruce J. "Pain, Power, and Personhood: Ascetic Behavior in the Ancient Mediterranean." In *Asceticism*, edited by Vincent Wimbush and Richard Valantasis, 162–77. New York: Oxford University Press, 1995.
Pourrat, Pierre. *Christian Spirituality*. Translated by W. H. Mitchell and S. P. Jacques. 4 vols. in 3. Westminster, MD: Newman, 1953.
Schechner, Richard. *Performance Theory*. Rev. and exp. ed. New York: Routledge, 1988.
Valantasis, Richard. "Constructions of Power in Asceticism." *Journal of the American Academy of Religion* 63 (1995) 775–821.

———. "Constructions of Power in Asceticism." In *The Making of the Self: Ancient and Modern Asceticism* 14–59. Eugene, OR: Cascade Books, 2008.

———. "Daemons and the Perfecting of the Monk's Body: Monastic Anthropology, Daemonology, and Asceticism." *Semeia* 58: *Discursive Formations, Ascetic Piety, and the Interpretation of Early Christian Literature*, edited by Vincent L. Wimbush, 47–79. Atlanta: Scholars, 1992.

———. *The Making of the Self: Ancient and Modern Asceticism*. Eugene, OR: Cascade Books, 2008.

———. "A Theory of Asceticism, Revised." In *The Making of the Self: Ancient and Modern Asceticism*, 101–16. Eugene, OR: Cascade Books, 2008.

———. "An Essay on Ministry and Culture: Integrating Ministry, Scholarship, and Spirituality." *Sewanee Theological Review* 36 (1993) 334–45.

Starred Material

* , 9 - Ministry...

** p 17 - Spirituality ...

* p 41 - ... development of the language of a corporate
         body...

*** p 53 Spiritually may also be understood

** p 62 "The function of reading the text is to reveal
        the presence of God in the community.

* * * p 69 what makes the sermon.

       , 79 "... ideas do not change people; experiences
        change people...

16593914R00079

Made in the USA
San Bernardino, CA
09 November 2014